STONESCAPING

A Guide to Using Stone in Your Garden

STONESCAPING

A Guide to Using Stone in Your Garden

Jan Kowalczewski Whitner

A Garden Way Publishing Book

Storey Communications, Inc.
Schoolhouse Road
Pownal, Vermont 05261

*The mission of Storey Communications is to serve our customers
by publishing practical information that encourages personal independence
in harmony with the environment.*

For Steve and Rob

Cover photograph by Grant Heilman

Cover design by Judy Eliason

Text design and production by Andrea Gray

Illustrations by Carl Kirkpatrick

Color section design and production by Judy Eliason

Copyright © 1992 by Jan Kowalczewski Whitner

The information in this book is true and complete to the best of our knowledge. All recommendations are made without guarantee on the part of the author or Storey Communications, Inc. The author and publisher disclaim any liability incurred with the use of this information. For additional information please contact Storey Communications, Inc., Schoolhouse Road, Pownal, Vermont 05261.

Garden Way Publishing was founded in 1973 as part of the Garden Way Incorporated Group of Companies, dedicated to bringing gardening information and equipment to as many people as possible. Today the name "Garden Way Publishing" is licensed to Storey Communications in Pownal, Vermont. For a complete list of Garden Way Publishing titles call 1-800-441-5700. Garden Way Incorporated manufactures products in Troy, New York, under the TROY-BILT® brand including garden tillers, chipper/shredders, mulching mowers, sicklebar mowers and tractors. For product information on any Garden Way Incorporated product, please call 1-800-345-4454.

Storey Publishing books are available for special premium and promotional uses and for customized editions. For further information, please call the Custom Publishing Department at 1-800-793-9396.

Printed in the United States by Courier

First Edition

20 19 18 17 16 15 14 13 12

Library of Congress Cataloging-in-Publication Data

Whitner, Jan Kowalczewski, 1949-
    Stonescaping : a guide to using stone in your garden / Jan Kowalczewski Whitner.
            p.   cm.
    Includes bibliographical references and index.
    ISBN 0-88266-756-4 (hc) — ISBN 0-88266-755-6 (pbk.)
    1. Stone in landscape gardening.   2. Rock gardens.   3. Building, Stone.   I. Title.
SB475.5.W45   1992
717—dc20
                                                                    91-55485
                                                                        CIP

CONTENTS

ACKNOWLEDGMENTS

I would like to thank Professor Jerome Silbergeld, Chair of the Art History Department at the University of Washington, for kindly reading the material that became Chapters 1 and 2; his expert comments and suggestions enriched the final manuscript, although it also contains material added after the draft that he read. I would also like to thank David Prager Branner of the Department of Asian Language and Literature at the University of Washington for correcting the spellings of Chinese names and terms. Needless to say, any errors in fact or interpretation in these chapters remain my own.

Thanks also to landscape architects Hoichi Kurisu and John Kenyon for sharing their insights into designing with stone, to the staff at the Elisabeth C. Miller Horticultural Library in Seattle, Washington, for their knowledgeable assistance, and to Pamela Gross and to my agent, Elizabeth Wales, for their good counsel and encouragement.

I would like to give special thanks to my mother, Doreen Kowalczewski, for her thoughtful perusal of the text, and to my husband, Steve Whitner, for his constant support, valuable suggestions, and careful reading of drafts.

INTRODUCTION

STONE SHAPES THE FACE OF THE EARTH.

Heaved up from miles inside its crust by earthquakes and erupting volcanoes, and then worn down below its surface by wind, water, and the slow, mysterious creep of glaciers, stone molds the earth's outermost layer during cycles that span eons. And in the mountain chains that rim oceans and split continents, the boulders that channel rivers, and the rocky outcroppings that groove hillsides or meadows, stone also cradles the soils, water, and plants that form the environment around us.

Stone can be used to play a comparable role in gardens. As a building material for walls, paths, and terraces, stone defines the boundaries and significant inner spaces of a garden. Used in ponds, streambeds, and rockeries, stone serves as a frame, softened and worn by time, for the garden's "living" elements, such as water, plants, sunlight, and shadows.

Beyond defining garden areas and framing garden elements, stone plays additional decorative and functional roles in a wide variety of garden types, roles based upon the philosophy and the sense of style which underlie the gardens themselves.

Stones have played richly allusive roles for many centuries in Chinese and Japanese gardens, for instance, where they are characterized as "the roots of heaven" and as fossilized dragon's bones. Stones are used to form the natural backbones of such gardens, in much the same way mountain ranges form the natural backbone of a continent, perhaps because stone's air of timeless stability and continuity appeals to cultures that value the same qualities in religion, art, and social interaction. Chinese and Japanese gardens most frequently use stone in its natural, uncut, form — a clear reflection of the value these cultures place on the aesthetic expression of the natural, in any artistic medium.

In traditional western gardens cut stones have played a predominately functional role as building blocks in the walls, terraces, steps, and paths that define such gardens and their inner spaces. "Wild" stone has played a less prominent role in western gardens than in Chinese and Japanese gardens, perhaps because the main thrust of the West's tradition has been to conquer and organize nature rather than emulate it. Certain decorative features in traditional western gardens, such as grottos, rockeries, fountains, and pools, use mixes of natural and cut stone, but these features usually function as sideshows. They are pockets where imagination is rather self-consciously allowed to run free, in contrast to the integral "hardscapes"— the walls, paths, and terraces — in which the garden's fundamental design unfolds and develops.

If stone has been used in such richly varied ways in the gardens of the past, how should we use it in gardens today? It depends, of course, upon our philosophy of what a garden ought to be, and how we expect to express that philosophy in tangible form in the landscape. The subject is a staple in twentieth-century garden writing, and while there may never be a consensus (and that's probably a good thing!), most gardeners would agree that there are several characteristics they find desirable for contemporary gardens. Let's see how stone features can be used to express them.

The first characteristic is that gardens must function as environments for people as well as for plants. This means that gardens should provide both comfort and sensory delight to their visitors. In today's gardens, where plots often are small and low-maintenance features are favored, stone can serve decorative and functional roles at the same time.

Small gardens need careful attention to detail to look their best, and the sum total of stone's sensory appeal — its textures, colors, shapes, shadows, and furrows — can be fully explored under such conditions. The rich visual interplay between cut stone, natural stone, gravel, pebbles, and sand, for instance, provides a never-ending variety of patterns for walls, paths, terraces, and all the other hardscapes that create a comfortable and functional environment for people outdoors.

Contemporary gardens also require a harmony of scale, "weight," and volume in their hardscapes — something that stone can provide with an entirely natural grace. And, on a practical note, stone features, once installed, are highly durable, with most requiring relatively little upkeep.

A second characteristic requires the contemporary garden to reflect, accurately and sensitively, the processes of nature. Most gardeners agree that contemporary gardens should highlight the curve of growth, fruition, and decay as nature itself expresses it, rather than showcasing manipulated environments, static compositions, and contrived associations of plants.

Here stone can act as a passive counterfoil to other elements in the garden, with its relationship to water and plants playing an especially evocative role. The quicksilver boundary between a pond and the stones that edge it, the supple spring of ornamental grasses against a solid bed of flagstones, the downward thrust of knotted tree roots plunging into mossy stones, and the slow crawl of ferns or sedums across the crevices of a dry stone wall: such details underline the relationship between what is living, and fleeting, in a garden and what is timelessly enduring.

Stonescaping is organized to acquaint readers with the history, design applications, and construction of stone features in the garden. Chapters 1 and 2 explore the way in which stone has been used in Chinese and Japanese gardens; Chapter 3 discusses how stone has been used in traditional western gardens; and Chapter 4 presents 20 design plans for using stone features in low-maintenance gardens, xeriscapes, small urban spaces, and renovations, as well as in a variety of traditional garden styles, such as cottage gardens, herb gardens, and formal gardens. Chapter 5 introduces readers to the varieties of stone available for garden construction, and how to acquire them, while Chapters 6 through 10 give detailed instructions for building stone paths, steps, walls, terraces, water features, rock gardens, and hypertufa plant containers.

I wrote *Stonescaping* to assist gardeners who have never worked with stone before to confidently create stone features as varied as those in the natural landscape and as imaginative as those in the gardens of the past — right in their own backyards. After all, when we use stone in our gardens, we are working with fragments of mountains and slivers of the ocean floors. What other kind of material binds our gardens so intimately to the very foundations of the earth?

PART I
The Asian Tradition

"Stones are the bones of heaven and earth" declared an early Chinese philosopher. His sense of rock's elemental role in the natural landscape has guided the way the Chinese and the Japanese have used it in their gardens ever since.

In fact, stones form the heart, as well as the bones, of Chinese and Japanese gardens. Moss-covered boulders set up as natural accents at a bend in the garden path, rocks trailing into a pond, and stepping stones wandering through a grove of bamboo: stone features play a subtle but structural role in Asian gardens that gives them a character distinct from all other garden styles.

The Chinese were the first to use stones in gardens, not only as building materials, but also as ornaments and symbols; their rich gardening tradition is explored in Chapter 1. Chapter 2 explains how the Japanese, who imported many gardening traditions from China, have developed the use of stones in gardens into an art which increasingly influences the contemporary West. Both the Chinese and Japanese traditions consider stone as a magical and evocative component in the designed landscape.

CHINESE GARDENS:
The Roots of Heaven

THE FIRST TIME WESTERNERS VISIT a Chinese garden, they are apt to feel confused, even disoriented, by what they see. In contrast to American or European gardens, which are designed as tranquil green retreats from an encroaching world, Chinese gardens seem like densely jumbled labyrinths of courtyards, buildings, and paths, all of them built without the occidental conventions of perspective and symmetry. In addition, westerners accustomed to the profusion of plants in their own gardens may find puzzling a Chinese garden's sparse, seemingly random plantings, as well as its obvious neglect of flowers as a major design element in the composition.

Instead, the jutting angles and surging curves of pavilions, paths, and latticed walls supply the Chinese garden's main visual interest. These features result in landscapes that may seem supercharged with hard surfaces and textures to visitors accustomed to the West's lush and leafy gardens.

But, to western eyes, perhaps the most surprising feature of all is the exotic way in which Chinese gardens display rocks and stones.

Some are filled with massive piles of eroded limestone, mottled grey and white like frozen clouds, that dominate their surroundings as if they were mountains set down into miniature landscapes. Paths twist through these heaps of boulders like narrow mountain roads, leading visitors past waterfalls, grottos, and stunted pines that cling to crevices in the rock. By wandering through these miniature mountain ranges up to their highest points, it's possible to gain a territorial view of the entire garden, or of the larger landscape outside the garden walls. These rock piles can create the illusion of compressed mountainscapes, complete with gorges, cliffs, and peaks, even within the narrow walls of a small courtyard garden.

Chinese gardens may feature single specimens of unusually shaped limestone or sandstone, displayed like outdoor sculptures. Over the centuries, the wind and water have carved these stones into abstract compositions, and they usually are positioned against whitewashed garden walls, where their hollowed, knotted textures show themselves to best advantage. Such special rocks have always served as an impetus to the Chinese creative imagination, with poets and painters finding continual inspiration in their swirling lines and in the everchanging play of light and shadow across their pitted and abraded surfaces.

Still other, "magical" rocks and stones are displayed as miniature tabletop specimens in elegant viewing pavilions, or in the scholars' libraries which traditionally are built to look out into the Chinese garden. The Chinese believe these thin shafts of precious jade or Yunnan green stone, mounted on marble bases, vibrate with currents that confer supernatural powers on those who touch them. Unusual veins or striations are particularly prized in such stones, since they are thought to serve as arteries, shrunk by age to a special spiritual potency, through which cosmic energy travels.

Whether they are used as miniature mountains, sculptures, or symbols of supernatural power, stone and rock have played distinctive roles in Chinese gardens for over twenty centuries, and their richly stratified layers of meaning reach far back into Chinese culture and tradition.

There are several reasons why. Since rock and gardens are intertwined in Chinese thought from an early period, perhaps the way to understand the Chinese fascination with rock and stone is to begin with the Chinese obsession with making gardens.

CHINA, MOTHER OF GARDENS

From the beginning, the tradition of making gardens plays a central role in Chinese society. One historian even claims that China's history is the history of making gardens, arguing that new ruling dynasties expressed their power and wealth primarily by establishing imperial gardens more magnificent than those of their predecessors. Tottering dynasties, on the other hand, often lost their grip on the empire through constructing ever more extravagant gardens, bankrupting their treasuries and the people's goodwill in the process.

But the Chinese make gardens for other purposes besides symbolizing political power. Sages, scholars, artists, and merchants also spent their best energies making private gardens, and they addressed spiritual and artistic questions central to Chinese culture in the process. In fact, it's hardly an exaggeration to say that from earliest times the Chinese have believed that all the arts — painting, poetry, philosophy, and literature — serve as stepping stones to the greatest art of all: making gardens.

Like poems and paintings, Chinese gardens evoke responses in viewers through the subtle manipulation of symbols and allusions, and every garden feature and scene has multiple layers of meaning for its viewers. For instance, visitors treading the stony paths of a garden rock pile might meditate on the monks and wise men who have wandered China's mountains for centuries in search of enlightenment and longevity. Approaching the "peaks" of this stylized mountain range, they may recall the immortal beings who are said to live on real mountaintops and then murmur to themselves a poem by Cao Zhi:

> I don my magic sandles and follow the magician
> Far off to Penglai Mountain.
> On the magic waters fly up pure white waves;
> The orchids and cassias reach the sky.
> Dark panthers roam below;
> Soaring cranes fly on top.
> Riding the wind I am suddenly drafted up
> And seem to see the hosts of the Immortals.[1]

Walking down the rock pile, they pass through a series of grottos, considered entryways to the Underworld, and then skirt a pond whose jade green surface is covered in lotuses, symbols of spiritual striving and rebirth. Later they stop to admire a specimen rock, whose furrows, folds, and knobs recall the stone before which landscape painter Mi Fu used to bow every morning and address as "elder brother," noting it displayed more constancy of character than he had ever found in human beings.

Thus Chinese gardens resonate with spiritual and aesthetic significance for visitors, and none of their features have richer symbolic meaning than rock and stones.

Whether featured in the imperial parks of emperors, the austere courtyard gardens of gentleman scholars, or the elegant pleasure grounds of rich merchants, rock and stone have always formed the bones of Chinese gardens. Let's look at the garden of an emperor, and then glance at a catalog of ornamental stones written by a gentleman scholar over a thousand years later, to understand both the rich cultural overlay which rock and stone contribute to the Chinese garden, and the pivotal role they have played in the development of the Chinese gardening tradition.

---

[1] Cao Zhi, *Worlds of Dust and Jade*, trans. George W. Kent (New York: Philosophical Library, 1969).

THE EARLIEST CHINESE GARDENS: IMPERIAL PARKS

When Han U di ascended the throne of the Chinese empire in 140 B.C., he inherited an immense pleasure garden, the Shanglin, which legend says extended for as much as 200 miles around the walls of his imperial palace, located near the present-day city of Xi'an.

Although Shanglin originated as a hunting preserve several hundred years before U di's day, over the course of time it came to symbolize, in miniature, the entire Chinese empire. Amid the park's natural landscape of hills, forests, lakes, and rivers, the emperors gathered prized flora and fauna from the four corners of China in order to represent the varied riches of their domain. By replicating the empire in compressed form within the boundaries of the imperial park, the emperors believed they were laying symbolic hold, by a kind of sympathetic magic, upon the real world outside the garden gates.

By U di's time, the Shanglin was considered a paradise on earth where, according to ancient chronicles, his Empress "could gaze about her from a high stone terrace. Amid the perfume of cassia trees, peacocks flocked together, monkeys screamed, kingfishers gathered, and phoenixes flew about."

U di's gardens were particularly rich in stone features. Early Chinese documents praise the Shanglin's magnificent scenic diversity, describing curving stone precipices rimming wide lakes, rocky gorges through which great rivers dashed, enormous cliffs made of twisted, furrowed stone, and even pebbles, winking and glinting in shallow streams like semiprecious stones.

GARDEN BONES AND HOLY MOUNTAINS

There are several reasons why stone features played such prominent roles in the Shanglin's landscape. One is that rock features dominate much of China's natural landscape in the form of mountains, cliffs, stone-choked gullies, and ravines. Since Chinese gardens are conceived as distillations or interpretations of the natural landscape, rock and stones have formed their structural "bones" from earliest times.

Another reason is that mountains and stones have been worshipped as divine beings from an early point in Chinese history. China's densest populations may live in the great river valleys, but the Chinese always have considered the cloud-hung mountains to be the country's spiritual center.

The early Chinese believed they were surrounded by sacred mountain ranges, with the holiest mountain of all, Mount T'ai, located near the Yellow River in Shandong Province. In the words of garden historian Maggie Keswick, mountains were considered "centers of cosmic energy, the conductors of that magic electricity which . . . flashed around their peaks, while the thunder roared and grumbled in the crags."[2] The mountains were said to generate the clouds draping their peaks, and so were seen as the source of rain and the empire's fertility. They have continued to inspire spiritual awe and regeneration in the poets, wise men, and ordinary pilgrims who wandered in them throughout China's history.

To U di and his predecessors at Shanglin, the imperial park's natural stone and rock features symbolized the emperors' vital link to the spiritual foundations of the empire: those mountains which, from the beginning, have dominated both the Chinese landscape and the Chinese imagination.

The Chinese fascination with rock and stones, therefore, began with an appreciation of their spiritual qualities and supernatural powers, and the venues in which they were first worshipped were mountain ranges. Later, the natural stone cliffs, gorges, and promontories in imperial parks came to symbolize the emperors' power over mountains and, by extension, the entire world.

By the Emperor Han U di's reign, manmade constructions using stone probably had already entered gardens as deliberate embellishments of the natural landscape. Because of his longing for immortality, however, U di was to add yet another type of stone construction — one which still plays a prominent role in Chinese and Japanese gardens over two thousand years later.

THE EMPEROR U DI'S ROCKY ISLANDS

Besides being sacred objects themselves, mountains were thought to be the haunts of supernatural beings. Chief among them were the Immortals, whom later Chinese artists often depict as wizened little demigods with the high, wrinkled foreheads and drooping earlobes typical of Chinese sages. Legend claimed they lived in a palace of jade with walls of gold in the great western mountain ranges near Tibet, where they dined on phoenix eggs, dragons' livers, and the peaches of immortality, which appear only once every six thousand years. The Immortals were also thought to inhabit the rocky Islands of the Dawn in the Eastern Sea near Japan, flying from one island to another on the backs of yellow cranes.

The desire for immortality had consumed emperors before Han U di. Over a hundred years earlier, Emperor Qin shihuang had built a palace to imitate the homes of celestial beings. Early accounts, in a richly imaginative mélange of fact and folklore, describe it as a 93-mile-long palace with countless chambers and pavilions winding up and down the foothills of a mountain, through which the emperor was believed to flutter about in the air, like a god. Legend also says Qin shihuang sent an expedition to the Eastern Sea to learn the secret of long life from the Im-

[2] *The Chinese Garden: History, Art & Architecture* (New York: St. Martin's, 1986).

mortals, but apparently they vanished into the clouds on their cranes long before the boats reached the islands.

U di decided to acquire the secret of longevity from the Immortals by making them a new home, an earthly paradise so tempting they would forsake their rocky islands and come to live in the emperor's gardens at a palace near the outskirts of Shanglin.

In order to snare the Immortals, U di decided to build them rocky islands in the middle of a lake, in imitation of their homes in the Eastern Sea. Swarms of workers barged earth and rock to the island sites, where they constructed naturalistic "mountains," grottos, waterfalls, and ponds. Later, rare plants and animals were introduced to the newly sculpted landscapes.

Once the islands were constructed, U di built a series of fairy palaces calculated to appeal to the Immortals. Legend says they featured "pillars of sweet-scented cassia wood, walls plastered with clay mixed with fragrant spices . . . curtains woven of swan feathers, and screens made of pearls and precious stones." Outside, brass filigree statues of phoenixes, symbols of longevity, turned in the garden breezes, while wide stone basins on pillars gathered dew, which Chinese folklore considered an elixir of immortality. We can imagine the emperor holding court in one of his island palaces, patiently, and, as it turned out, fruitlessly, watching for the Immortals to glide across the horizon to their splendid new homes.

U di's association of rock piles with the homes of supernatural beings has continued to influence Chinese and Japanese garden design to the present day. Because of this evocative association, an atmosphere of mystery still clings even to such modest garden features as a single rock set in the still pond of a private garden.

MINIATURE MOUNTAINS

Although the beginnings of private gardens are lost in the shadows of early Chinese history, by the fourth century A.D. government officials, artists, and merchants were creating gardens of their own. China's various regions exhibit vast differences in terrain, vegetation, and artistic expression, and garden historians know far more about some regional garden styles than others. In the garden styles that can be documented, however, private gardens adapt themes of the imperial parks from a point early in their development, using stone features to express them.

As previously mentioned, the imperial parks were considered models, on a reduced scale, of the larger world, with rock mounds representing mountains and ponds or lakes evoking oceans. Private gardens now began to replicate the world on a still smaller scale, making individual rocks symbolize entire mountains and pebble-strewn streams represent mighty rivers. These private gardens used stone features on a minute scale for several reasons.

One was the perennial enthusiasm among educated and urban Chinese for the idea of returning to nature. Poems, paintings, and philosophical literature expressed the joys of living the natural life in a pastoral, even wild, setting. For those Chinese tied to city life, their gardens came to represent the natural landscape and the life of solitude. Yet, because Chinese cities are densely populated and living space within them is always at a premium, garden designers had to learn ways to represent the wilderness on a miniature scale.

Since mountains, rock, and stone were considered the bones of the natural landscape, it was considered quite essential to feature them in every garden, however small. Therefore, garden designers devised ways to construct "false mountains" of piles of rock and earth for small urban gardens, paying careful attention to establishing a harmonious scale between them and other garden features. Such rock hills were usually built in tandem with ponds, and the design combination of quicksilver water and immutable stone remains as the heart of the Chinese garden even today.

At the same time artists were developing gardens that served as "embodied poems" and "three-dimensional paintings" — meticulously laid-out landscapes as carefully composed and executed as a poem or a drawing. Elegance and refinement of scale also were characteristic of these gardens, and often individual stones of exceptional beauty or bizarre appearance were set up as focal points for the entire composition.

By the sixth century A.D. the passion for using stone in private gardens was well established; the writings of a gentleman scholar of the twelfth century document how richly the tradition of stone lore developed in subsequent years.

THE HERMIT OF THE CLOUDY FOREST

About 1131 A.D. Du Wan, a descendant of poets and statesmen, a self-described hermit, and a confirmed petromaniac, wrote a book about stones and rocks called *Stone Catalogue of Cloudy Forest*. Despite its plain and practical style, Du Wan's fascination with ornamental rocks and stones permeates the book, giving us insight into what sparked the Chinese imagination about the use of stone in the natural landscape and in the garden.

The introduction to the *Catalogue* explains that studying stones purifies the imagination, with the book's translator adding that, "for the gentleman a stone, as a microcosmic mountain, suggests nobility, patience, stability, seclusion, and the virtuous contemplation of nature."[3] If we add to this an aesthetic delight in the

[3]Edward H. Shafer, from the introduction to *Stone Catalogue of Cloudy Forest*, by Du Wan, trans. E. H. Shafer (Berkeley and Los Angeles: University of California Press, 1961).

shapes, textures, and colors of rock, we begin to understand the enthusiasm with which Du Wan traveled all over twelfth-century China, combing mountains and rivers famous for their native rock.

Du Wan lists 116 different kinds of rock in the *Catalogue*, placing them into two major categories — either as ornamental or as practical (i.e., in making handcrafts, structures, even cosmetics) in use. The heart of the book, however, lies in its first chapter, which describes both the appearance of ornamental rocks and stones and how they are to be used in the garden.

Du Wan says that ornamental rocks should be selected for use in gardens according to several criteria. One concerns the type of hollows and perforations a stone displays: since a form of cosmic energy resides in them, a stone with numerous and deep perforations is to be especially prized. The skeletal structure or overall shape of the rock is also important, because the Chinese believe that an object's structure, or bones, reveals its inmost character. Lastly, the ribbing and striations on a stone's surface are significant, since they represent its veins, the conduits of spiritual power.

Rock and stone seem to spring to life in Du Wan's vivid descriptions. He says, for instance, that *lingbi*, a kind of pumice found in the mountains of Anhui Province, comes in shapes and textures that remind him of "clouds and vapors, the sun and moon, or the figure of Buddha." Du Wan notes that *lingbi* stones, especially those colored ashy white or coral, make good chimes because of the rich, deep notes that ring out when you strike them, and he recommends they be used in the garden in miniature arrangements to suggest rugged mountains," with peaks and tors, craggy and precipitious, perforated and cavernous."

Du Wan also lists the most celebrated type of rock used in Chinese gardens — the limestone monoliths dredged from the depths of Lake T'ai near present-day Suzhou. Termed "the roots of heaven" and "flower stones," these *t'ai hu* rocks display all the qualities most appreciated by Chinese stone connoisseurs. They vary in color from ash to oyster to charcoal grey, and their surfaces dip into delicate hollows and swell out into rough knobs. (Experts speculate that the *t'ai hu* rocks originally were limestone and sandstone aggregates. They theorize that when the turbulent waters of Lake T'ai eroded the sandstone pockets, the remaining limestone assumed its characteristic fantastic shape.) Individual *t'ai hu* specimens range from relatively modest-sized rocks to ones with a height of ten feet or more, and they are generally set on bases where they can be displayed and viewed from all sides, like sculpture. Chinese viewers see coiling dragons, lunging tigers, or swirling clouds in their shadowed contours, and personalize them to the extent of giving individual stones names and pedigrees.

Perhaps *t'ai hu* rocks capture the Chinese imagination because they are massive yet delicate, immutable yet fluid, unchanging yet dynamic: with such qualities they illustrate the paradoxical spirit which the best Chinese gardens embody.

T'ai hu rocks were considered rare and valuable by Du Wan's day, and emperors filled the imperial gardens with the most exquisite examples to be found in the empire. Already there was a booming cottage industry for "improving" such rocks. The methods included grinding, smoking, polishing, and dying, as well as improving their shapes with hand tools and then setting them under waterfalls to gain an aged and pitted-looking surface quickly. Similarly, garden "mountains" were glued together from numerous small stones, and skillful craftsmen cantilevered boulders at precipitous angles to simulate mountain cliffs and gorges.

ROCK'S ESSENTIAL FUNCTION IN CHINESE GARDENS

These contrivances point out that Chinese gardens are highly artificial environments which interpret, rather than duplicate, the natural landscape. Although cut stone does play a purely functional role in them when used in walls, steps, and terraces, it's the symbolic use of natural stone in rock piles or as individual specimens that gives Chinese gardens their distinctive style. Stone's use in such features is always dramatic, with its colors, textures, and lines providing stimulating contrasts to the whitewashed walls, rammed earth floors, and scattered plants surrounding it.

Above all, rocks and stones are used in Chinese gardens to underscore their function as compressed and distilled versions of the larger landscape: in this sense, to the Chinese, stone evokes and typifies the skeleton of the entire earth.

CHAPTER 2

JAPANESE GARDENS:
Across the Eastern Sea

WHILE JAPANESE GARDENERS ALSO USE STONE as the foundation of their gardens, the results are quite different both in function and appearance. Where the Chinese tend to pile rocks on top of one another in large heaps, in Japanese gardens they most often are used individually, or in small groups, with each stone remaining firmly anchored to the earth. Rocks in Chinese gardens seem to thrust out like spiny mountain ranges or lunging mythical beasts; in Japanese gardens they appear settled down into the ground, like bones poking through the earth's crust wherever it has worn thin. And there is a solidity and serenity in the way stones inhabit their spaces in Japanese gardens which stands in sharp contrast to the exuberant, almost restless quality of stone features in many Chinese gardens.

As a design element, stone also functions differently in the two garden styles. The Chinese value stone features for their bizarre appearance and allusive qualities, using them as exclamation points in the grammar of a garden composition. In Japanese gardens, rocks and stones are meant to look entirely natural, and they are used to harmoniously bind together all the components — slope, water, plants — of a particular site. Thus, while the Chinese use *t'ai hu*, pumice, and other unusual varieties of stone in elaborate arrangements meant to represent (but not to replicate) the natural landscape, the Japanese use granites, gneiss, schists, and other naturally aged and weathered rocks in groups arranged to look naturally understated.

Finally, rather than representing entire "mountains" or "islands" in the abstract, as in Chinese gardens, stone's main function in a Japanese garden — Zen rock and gravel gardens aside — is usually to bind the landscape more closely to its particular setting and to evoke the spirit of a particular site. They often do this by recreating some aspect of the larger landscape within the garden. For instance, several large river rocks and some rounded pebbles established in the dry curves of a garden hillock in a Japanese garden may evoke for viewers the river and waterfalls streaming down the mountainside right outside the garden gate.

A look at the history of the Japanese garden explains why stone's role evolved in this way.

LIVING STONES AND "PURE PLACES"

Like China, Japan is a country of mountains and rocks. Chains of mountains wander down the centers of its four main islands, and their coastlines are rimmed by rocky bays, cliffs, and islands. Seventy-five percent of the land is mountainous, and the vast majority of the population live in the relatively few coastal plains and river valleys.

Rock has always been associated with the mysterious and inaccessible mountains in the Japanese imagination, and from an early date special stones and rocks were considered manifestations of divine vitality. In fact, tradition credits rocks with growth and change, as if they were living things: pebbles were believed to have evolved over the course of centuries into the massive boulders which litter the Japanese landscape. The early Japanese also believed that stones were the bones of dragons and that some earth-dwelling deities inhabited special rocks.

In accordance with the early Japanese religious practices termed Shinto, sites on which such special rocks rested were made into "pure places," natural clearings that were cordoned off from intruders. Some early Shinto shrines encompassed several "pure places" scattered over an acre or more, with paths of gravel and water features, such as streams and ponds, connecting them together. Worshippers strolled from one "pure place" to another within the shrine complex, their spiritual and aesthetic responses to the holy objects — primarily rocks and stones — intermingling with and reinforcing one another.

Both the purpose and the layout of these Shinto shrines have served as models for Japanese gardens from their beginnings up until the present time. The idea that gardens are special areas set apart for spiritual refreshment and regeneration, coupled with the concept of creating several different "scenes" within a garden complex, remain basic components of Japanese garden design today.

When Korean and Chinese travelers introduced the idea of making gardens to Japan in the seventh century A.D., the emperors and their courts received it enthusiastically. Chinese garden styles influenced the first Japanese gardens ever built; they were rock-hill gardens reminiscent of U di's Islands of the Immortals near Shanglin. Thus, the native Japanese reverence for rock was combined with imported Chinese design ideas to create Japanese gardens whose foundations, from the earliest point in their development, were made of rock and stone.

"A WAY TO PUT THE HEART IN ORDER"

In the centuries that followed, large public and private gardens built on the Chinese rock-hill model used stone and rock not only to represent mountains and islands, but also to symbolize new religious concepts. The early Shinto identification of rocks as manifestations of divine energy was joined, after the introduction of Buddhism to Japan in the sixth century, with the idea of using rocks and stones to express Buddhist beliefs.

For example, a group of three rocks set together in the corner of a garden might represent the relationship between humans, heaven, and earth — a cosmological model traced out in stone. Or, drawing on popular religious folklore, a rock representing the celestial boat, which legend claimed the gods filled with precious stones and floated down to earth, might be placed near a cascade in a pond. This fusion between rock's spiritual and aesthetic roles remains a prime characteristic in Japanese gardens to the present day.

In fact, there is a saying in Japan that learning to set stones well in the garden is a kind of spiritual exercise, a way to "put the heart in order," and certain rock shapes traditionally are used to evoke particular moods and emotional responses in the garden viewer (see Table 2–1 on p. 20).

By the thirteenth century gardening manuals had developed rules for selecting and grouping rocks, and these conventions became so formal over time that taboos began to surround the setting of stones. One medieval gardening manual, for instance, warns that using a rock against its nature, i.e., placing one with horizontal striations in a vertical position, transforms it into a "stone of revengeful spirits," which will bring misfortune to the garden it is placed in, as well as to the garden's owner.

Today, Japanese garden designers still approach siting stones in the landscape with the same kind of extreme sensitivity. It's not uncommon, if a new house and its garden are to be constructed at the same time, for the garden designer to bury all the large rocks to be used in the garden on site, before the house is built. Once the house is completed, work on the garden begins by resurrecting the buried rocks from the earth.

Although this sequence is practical — it's usually easier to uncover large rocks on site than to attempt to bring them in after the lot is built up — the Japanese garden designer continues to find it satisfying, on a symbolic level, to begin a new garden by heaving rock up from inside the earth.

After the twelfth century, the Japanese developed new, distinctly native garden styles that were less influenced by Chinese models. Characteristically, these new types of gardens were smaller in scale than Chinese gardens, and so each element within them — especially stone — bore proportionately more loaded functions and meanings. During the next several centuries, three major new garden styles evolved, and rock and stone played distinctive roles in them all.

Beginning with the Chinese-influenced rock-hill style, let's take a look at how stone and rock are used in each and then consider some lessons western gardeners can adapt from them when making stone features in their own backyards.

Rock-Hill Gardens

Rock-hill gardens take their design cues from the natural landscape. Just as rivers course down hills into valleys, where they widen into lakes, so manmade waterfalls and streams wander down mounds of rocks and earth to ponds in rock-hill gardens. Rock's major function in these gardens is to create changes in heights and levels, as hills and mountains do in the natural landscape. The rock hills usually do this by forming the back perimeters of the garden and asymmetrically rimming a pond, which functions as the central garden feature.

Stones and rocks usually play a naturalistic role in rock-hill gardens, replicating the stony crags or rocky outcroppings seen in the Japanese mountains and foothills. Generally, large rounded stones and low flat-headed stones are used in the rock hills, with occasional tall, vertical rocks used for accents near the "peaks" of the mounds. Tall, vertical rocks can also be set at the point where streams or waterfalls first spring out of the rock hills, in order to suggest rocky gorges or stone cliffs high in the mountains. Low, flat stones are used around the pond to enhance its horizontal sweep of lines, while island rocks, either individual specimens or small rock and earth mounds planted with low-growing shrubs and dwarf trees, symbolize the homes of the Immortals.

Although rock-hill gardens generally are the most spacious Japanese garden style, in practice they can be built to small sites, too. Large scenes can be presented on a reduced scale, so long as a proper balance between the various garden elements — rock, water, and plants — is maintained. Because rocks and stones are the main element used to establish the scale on a site, they should be in proper proportion to each other, as well as balancing with the other garden features.

Dry Landscapes

Dry landscapes were developed by monk-gardeners as an aid to meditation after the introduction of Zen Buddhism to Japan in the twelfth century. In contrast to the spacious, naturalistic rock-hill gardens, dry landscape gardens are small, flat, austere in mood, and usually feature only rocks and raked gravel. Often surrounded by plain, whitewashed walls that provide them with a blank backdrop, the rocks and stones in these dry landscapes form abstract patterns that allow the imagination to run free. Generally, large rounded rocks are used as the main stone feature in a dry landscape, with low, flat-headed rocks grouped about them in a kind of dynamic repose. Occasionally, tall vertical rocks are added to the composition for contrast. The overall mood established by these rock groups is one of focused and balanced energy. Because rocks — and the play of light and shadow between them — create the primary visual interest in dry landscape gardens, the spatial relationship between individual specimens or groups assumes great importance.

Rocks are often used in dry landscapes to represent islands in a sea of gravel, with patterns raked into the gravel to resemble waves and currents. And dry streambeds, fashioned from rounded river rocks and carefully laid "rivers" of pebbles, are used in any style of Japanese garden when the spirit of water, rather than its real presence, is wanted in the landscape.

Tea Gardens

Tea gardens are carefully landscaped settings for the tea ceremony. The garden style began in the sixteenth century as a simple pathway to the tea house itself, but gradually evolved into a refined garden featuring subdued plantings, rocks selected for their elegant shapes, colors, and textures, and cut stone lanterns and water basins. Large, rounded stones, reclining stones, and low, flat-headed stones most often are used in tea gardens because their shapes contribute a mood of serenity to the setting.

The tea garden also encourages a tranquil state of mind in viewers by focusing their attention on subtle garden details: the play of dappled sunlight over moist pools of moss, and the gleam of water puddling on a stepping stone.

While tea gardens feature stones as beautiful objects in themselves, they also are used to reveal the essence of other garden components. The fluid grace of water cupped in a stone basin contrasts the essential qualities of both water and stone in a quietly satisfying way. And the transitory beauty of an azalea bloom is enhanced by the solid mass of a nearby boulder. Although stone complements and balances plants in all styles of Japanese gardens, this design technique reaches its subtle perfection in the well-made tea garden.

Stroll Gardens

Stroll gardens developed in the seventeenth century as free interpretations of the rock-hill gardens, but they offer several innovations in design and purpose. Earlier garden styles, with their close connections to the ancient "pure places," functioned as static compositions which viewers contemplated from verandahs or viewing spots at designated points in the garden. In contrast, stroll gardens function simply as pleasure grounds, and they invite viewers to enter the garden and move through it. This garden style gradually reveals its scenery around each new bend in the path, like an unfolding scroll painting, and stone features are designed to be seen from all angles in the landscape.

Stroll gardens use a mix of natural stone, such as rock hills and boulders, as well as cut stone features — walls, terraces, steps, and bridges — to define separate areas in the garden. Because stroll gardens use stone in ways that are most similar to the way western gardens use it, a look at how landscape architect John Kenyon of Seattle adapts Japanese stroll garden design principles to the American landscape will provide a fund of ideas to western gardeners. (Kenyon's stroll garden is illustrated in Chapter 4 under "A Garden Renovation Using Stone," p. 56.)

A JAPANESE APPROACH TO USING STONES IN GARDENS

The Japanese prefer to use rocks with dense textures and aged patinas, such as granite, schist, and gneiss, in their gardens. Although the variety of natural rock shapes is infinite, five major types are recognized for the purposes of garden design. (See Table 2–1, next page).

Placement in the Site

Rocks and stones are used in Japanese garden features according to their roles in the natural landscape. River rocks, for instance, are used in garden streams and waterfalls, while tall vertical stones collected from a mountainside represent cliffs or promontories in the garden.

The fundamental aim in placing stones in Japanese gardens is to make them look as natural a part of the landscape as possible.

Although in practice most experts suggest burying between one-third and one-half of a stone's bulk in order to achieve this look, every stone's lines and dynamics are different, and each requires experimentation before a final set is made. Probably the best rule of thumb is to bury a rock at its point of maximum girth.

Setting Stones

The Japanese gardener sees each stone as an individual, whose full character is only revealed when its "best face" and "top" are sited correctly. It usually isn't particularly difficult to determine where they are: the best face is the one that features the most beautiful veining, furrows, and colors, and is sited so that it faces

Table 2–1
ROCK TYPES

ROCK TYPES	EVOKED QUALITIES AND MOODS	APPEARANCE	FUNCTION
Tall, vertical rock	Austerity, determination	Taller than wide at the point where it enters the ground. Has a vertical thrust, with a head that is somewhat pointed.	Frequently used as an accent near the top of a rock hill, and as a major stone in a waterfall composition. Evokes mountains and cliffs.
Large, rounded rock	Warmth, authority	Wider than tall at the point where it enters the ground, usually with a height-to-width ratio somewhere around 1:1.5. Often features a rounded head.	Probably the most frequently used stone type in a Japanese garden; often used as the centerpiece of a group of rocks. Used on hills, in or near ponds, and as an accent to a tall, vertical stone. Evokes rocky fields and stony outcroppings.
Low, flat-headed rock	Stability, placidity	Usually less than a foot high, and of almost any width. Always has a more or less flat head.	Used most frequently as a stepping stone or an informal step.
Arching rock	Activity, force	A little less tall than a large, rounded stone. Arches to one side with a decided thrust. Vertical in nature.	Frequently used when the eye needs to be pulled in a specific direction, for example, toward the centerpiece in a group of rocks, or around a bend in a garden path.
Reclining rock	Peacefulness, serenity	Always wider than high, with an irregular slope upwards to one side. Horizontal in nature.	Most frequently used as a companion to a large, rounded stone, as a natural base to a rock hill, and as an island in a pond.

the major incoming line of view. The top is the edge that forms the stone's most visually satisfying crown, once its best face has been determined.

Grouping Rocks and Stones

The Japanese traditionally group rocks together asymmetrically and in odd numbers in order to evoke nature's ragged order. Rocks to be used in groups are matched for certain features, such as color, texture, and pattern of striation, and contrasted for other qualities, such as size and shape. The main idea in grouping stones together is to set up an interesting balance between their matched and contrasting features.

SEQUENCE FOR GROUPING ROCKS AND STONES

The traditional sequence for composing rock groups starts with a central stone, usually a tall, vertical or a large, rounded one, and then adds a second stone which balances and accents the first one. Each new rock added to the composition should maintain the balance and harmony of the core group, while developing a new facet in the overall design (see Figure 2–1, p. 22).

For example, if a large, rounded stone **(a)** is selected as the central stone for a rock group, then placing a lower recliner **(b)** to its left, so the recliner's ascending line leads the eye toward the top of the central stone, will balance the composition. A low, flat-headed stone **(c)** placed at the front of the group adds both foreground depth and stability to the design.

If a tall, vertical rock **(d)** complemented by an arching stone **(e)** to its right is sited near, but not adjacent to the first rock group, then an interesting relationship is created among all five individual stones, as well as between the two groups. As this sequence illustrates, building group compositions stone by stone ensures a cohesive overall design, as well as visually satisfying relationships between individual stones and groups.

Mossy Rocks

Mossy rocks are especially prized features in Japanese gardens; often they are wrapped in rags to preserve their "patina" while being transported to a new site. Japanese gardeners traditionally "feed" mossy rocks by sprinkling them with water in which rice has been rinsed. (The rice polishings contain a nourishing starch.)

Here are some ideas for growing mosses on your garden stones:

- *If mosses grow naturally in your region.* Collect a moss-covered stone from a site that has similar light and moisture conditions to those found on the new site in your garden. Position the mossy stone near your new, "naked" stones,

Figure 2–1. Sequence for grouping rocks in Japanese gardens.

sprinkle the stones with a mixture of sugar and water, keep them moist thereafter, and wait for nature to take its course.

- *If you want to hurry the process, or mosses need some encouragement in your region.* Scrape a small patch of moss from a stone that has the same levels of light and moisture as your newly positioned garden stones. Place the moss on top of a clean piece of cheesecloth that has been laid over a flat of good potting soil. Keep the flat moist and in shade. When the moss establishes itself and starts to spread over the cheesecloth, cut the cheesecloth into small pieces and transfer them to the bases of the stones. Be sure to keep the stones receptively moist with a sugar and water solution while the moss spreads.

- *If you live in a hot, dry region where most mosses cannot live.* Consider planting sandwort (*Arenaria* spp.) at the base of the stones instead of moss to achieve a similar effect.

PART II
The Western Tradition

For centuries the Chinese and Japanese have maintained virtually unbroken traditions of revering mountains as centers of spiritual power and of conferring symbolic significance on the use of natural stone in gardens. During a comparable span of time, the West developed ambivalent, even conflicting attitudes toward mountains, and it has used stone in gardens in ways distinctly different from the Asian tradition.

The Chinese and Japanese traditionally value mountains as symbols of a natural world they find both holy and transcendent, but well into the eighteenth century most Europeans saw mountains as symbols of a natural landscape they considered a desolate and frightening wilderness. Perhaps as a result, little spiritual or cultural significance attached to the use of stone in its natural state in western gardens before the eighteenth century. Instead, cut stone was used almost exclusively, with its functional and decorative values fully exploited in walls, terraces, fountains, paths, and other garden features.

Chapter 3 surveys the history of western attitudes toward stone both in the natural landscape and in gardens, attitudes derived from the cultures of the ancient Middle East, the classical world, and early Europe.

Chapter 4 then illustrates how stone features are being adapted from earlier European and Asian gardening traditions to create attractive, innovative, and practical gardens today.

EUROPEAN GARDENS:
From Paradise to Eden

THERE WAS A TRADITION OF REVERENCE for stone and rock as spiritually powerful natural objects in the early western world: rocks bundled in hides with talismans and other religious paraphernalia thousands of years old have been found in caves all over Europe and western Asia. And the numerous scatterings of megaliths and dolmens throughout western Europe remind us that peoples in that region were alive to the spiritual associations of stone and rock in the landscape from an early period.

This reverence for rock extended to mountains. The Greeks, Romans, and Celts believed their gods lived near the peaks of mountains or in caves under them, while Judaism, Christianity, and Islam designated mountains as holy ground — the places most natural for God and humans to interact.

But this reverence alternated with a decided undercurrent of fear. In Scandinavia, for instance, frost giants, trolls, and dwarfs were thought to haunt mountain peaks, and in other parts of Europe folk beliefs made mountains the homes of witches, werewolves, and the souls of the damned. In a similar vein, western literature and paintings from early in the medieval period up until the eighteenth century usually portray natural stone features as alien and threatening terrain, with little intrinsic beauty. As late as the last half of the seventeenth century, Thomas Burnet, an English traveler to the Alps, could write "[the mountains] have neither Form nor Beauty, nor Shape, nor Order. There is nothing in Nature more shapeless and ill-figured than an old Rock or a Mountain."[1]

[1]Quoted in *Sacred Mountains of the World* by Edwin Bernbaum (San Francisco: Sierra Club Books, 1990), p. 121.

By the eighteenth century, as the Romantic movement burgeoned, an appreciation of the informal beauty of the natural landscape and the grandeur of natural stone features began to develop. At the same time, garden designers were starting to appreciate the aesthetic role uncut stone could play in their designs, although the expression of such an appreciation was confined, for the most part, to the creation of naturalistic water cascades or stony outcroppings in the wilder parts of a garden. In creating such natural stone features, we might say, western gardeners were beginning to introduce a kind of wildness into the garden, a wildness which previously had been excluded in part through the medium of cut and sculpted stone.

Nineteenth-century gardens returned to a geometric formality in their design, and it was not until the development of new garden styles in the present century that natural stone features began once again to play a significant role in the garden.

Our survey of the way stone is used in western gardens begins with the gardens of the Middle East and Rome.

PARADISE GARDENS OF THE MIDDLE EAST

The western gardening tradition has its roots deep in the Middle East, where gardens have always been seen as verdant oases of water and lush plants, protected by walls from the threatening and desolate wilderness outside. Natural rocks, as reminders of that stony, inhospitable terrain, played virtually no role in such gardens, but cut stone was used from an early date to construct the pavilions, pools, and other features which composed their hardscapes.

Water — splashing, purling, cooling water — was the paramount feature of these early paradise gardens, which were being built with considerable splendor in Mesopotamia by the sixth century B.C. Now that archaeologists have excavated garden sites all over the Middle East — ranging from palace pleasure grounds built by Cyrus the Great in south-central Iran around 550 B.C. to the sumptuous gardens of Mughal India created over two thousand years later — it is apparent that consistent design features using stone characterize all paradise gardens.

Traditionally, two carved stone watercourses, intersecting at the garden's center, divided the site into quarters. The courses, often made from cut limestone blocks, symbolized the division of the world by the four rivers of life, which the peoples of the ancient Middle East believed encompassed and nourished the entire world. The watercourses were bordered by formal rows of cypresses and fruit trees, and the garden quarters functioned as planting beds, where roses, tulips, and ornamental shrubs grew. Householders loved to sit in their gardens in the evening, after the heat of the day had passed, to enjoy the burble of water and the scent of flowers and herbs.

In Cyrus the Great's palace gardens the gravity-fed limestone watercourses were interrupted at regular intervals by small stone water basins, which seem to have served as early prototypes for pleasure pools. The stone watercourses served a purely decorative role, since water for irrigation was supplied by nearby drainage ditches.

Over the centuries, as paradise gardens became more elaborate, octagonal pools made of pure white marble, or pavilions with stone cupolas as delicate as spun sugar, capped the point where the watercourses crossed at the center of the garden. And because sparkling water continued to be the dominating design component, fountains and water chutes made of stone also played significant roles in garden architecture.

The geometric formality that stone watercourses imposed on the earliest paradise gardens continues to characterize all gardens designed with Middle Eastern influences. As a result of Islam's expansion through North Africa into Spain in the early Middle Ages, the formal air and symmetrical lines of the paradise gardens influenced the design of European gardens, from medieval walled gardens to the stunning pleasure grounds of seventeenth-century France and Italy.

STONE FEATURES IN ROMAN AND MEDIEVAL GARDENS

The few detailed descriptions we have of Roman garden architecture consistently stress that is was both precise and formal, with straight lines, right angles, and semicircles dominating the typical site. Like the enclosed paradise gardens of the Middle East many Roman gardens, especially the courtyard gardens in cities, were built as extensions of the house with stone columns, colonnades, and loggias blurring the distinctions between inside and outside living spaces.

Roman garden design carefully balanced planting schemes — such as hedges and topiaries made of box, rosemary, and other evergreens — with aquaducts, terraces, pools, and fountains made of cut stone. In addition, stone statues and large vases made from stone and pottery served as garden ornaments.

With the fall of Rome, gardening retreated behind the stone walls of the monasteries. Although monastery gardens were meant primarily to be useful, with square or rectangular raised borders planted in medicinal herbs and flowers, contemporary descriptions make them seem attractive, and even ornamental. In a typical monastery garden, fruit trees hung over the enclosing stone walls, cooing doves rimmed marble fountains dripping water into shallow pools below, and gravel paths, which crossed each other in the center to define the symmetrical planting beds, echoed the stone watercourses of earlier paradise gardens.

By the thirteenth century, the enclosed gardens in palaces and manors throughout western Europe featured not only stone walls,

(continued on page 35)

TOP: *The aesthetic and spiritual power of stone has occupied a central place in Chinese garden tradition for thousands of years. This courtyard, at the Dr. Sun Yat-Sen Classical Chinese Garden in Vancouver, features a composition of limestone t'ai hu rocks. The imaginative appeal of such a setting stems from the paradoxical character of the stones themselves: massive yet delicate, unchanging yet dynamic. The result is a landscape in miniature that seeks to interpret rather than duplicate nature.* Photo courtesy of Dr. Sun Yat-Sen Classical Chinese Garden.

ABOVE: *Since ancient times, ponds have been used in Japanese gardens to represent the ocean with its rocky islands and coastline. The tall vertical rocks in this photograph, from Nijo Castle in Kyoto, are particularly evocative of cliffs or headlands facing a placid sea.*

LEFT: *Gravel paths are appropriate to a wide variety of garden styles, including natural and Japanese. At Nomura Villa in Kyoto, the dark gravel is enhanced both overhead and underfoot by colorful autumn foliage.*

RIGHT: *Spacing individual stepping stones in an asymmetric, rhythmic pattern encourages a leisurely pace and creates an interesting, natural-looking path.*

BELOW: *Stepping-stone paths can work particularly well in natural settings. This narrow woodland path invites visitors to leisurely enjoy the flowering shrubs and foliage on either side.*

LEFT: *Mortared flagstone paths are well suited to high-traffic areas adjacent to the house. This informal flagstone walk skirts a bed of columbine* (Aquilegia canadensis).

LEFT: *Dry stone walls (those laid without mortar) can support a variety of plants. Here, mother-of-thyme* (Thymus praecox) *creeps over the top of an informal wall while saxifrage* (Saxifraga paniculata 'Brevifolia') *grows in its "pockets."*

ABOVE: *In cold climates, siting stone walls so that they face south or west can create sunny pockets that retain warmth and encourage early-flowering plants like these spring bulbs.*

LEFT: *This ashlar (cut stone) wall serves double duty, as a formal boundary for a neatly clipped lawn and to enclose a bed of ornamental shrubs.*

TOP RIGHT: *Terraces can serve a variety of functions — as "outdoor rooms" for entertaining or dining or as viewing points from which to enjoy the garden. This quiet corner terrace is paved with formal flagstones interplanted with sedum, thyme, and tansy.*

BOTTOM RIGHT: *Small crushed rock packs down well and provides an attractive and durable surface for places with heavy foot traffic, as around this formal vegetable and herb garden.*

ABOVE: *A central stone font surrounded by boxwood, rosemary, sage, rue, and southernwood captures the spirit of a monastic herb garden in medieval Europe.*

30

ABOVE: *Formal western gardens of the Renaissance period and later imposed a sense of order, harmony, and proportion on the landscape by using cut stone in features such as paths, pools, and walls. This garden room at Hestercombe in Surrey features stone borders that highlight its formal lines and angles.*

LEFT: *The still waters of a small pond, edged with rocks and tufts of ornamental grasses* (Miscanthus *'Morning Light'*), *bring a sense of depth and serenity to this Maryland garden.*

TOP RIGHT: *The reflecting eye of this moss-covered raised pool softens and enlivens the formal stonework of the surrounding terrace.*

BELOW LEFT: *A flight of water-stairs channels water gently into a rock-rimmed pond.*

ABOVE: *When grouping stones, Japanese designers strive for a balance between the matching and contrasting features of the individual rocks. Each new rock added to the composition should maintain the balance and harmony of the core group, while introducing a new facet into the overall design.*

LEFT: *Low, creeping plants and ornamental grasses complement the colors of the stone in this naturalistic rock-hill garden.*

TOP: *An informal path of stepping stones curves past a Zen garden grouping of specimen rocks at the Portland Japanese Garden in Portland, Oregon.*

BOTTOM LEFT: *A rockery creates the perfect environment for many native and drought-tolerant plant species like the yarrow* (Achillea) *and New Zealand flax* (Phormium tenax *'Bronze Baby'*) *found in this Santa Barbara, California, garden.*

BOTTOM RIGHT: *A dry streambed made of rounded river rocks can be used in any landscape where the spirit of water, rather than its actual presence, is desired.*

ABOVE: *A flight of weathered stone steps winds next to a planting of basket-of-gold* (Aurinia saxatalis), *sedum* (Sedum spathulifolium), *and aubrieta* (Aubrieta deltoidea).

TOP RIGHT: *Asian gentians, flowering freely in a stone trough at Rodmarton Manor in Gloucestershire. The popularity of stone troughs among English gardeners led to the development of hypertufa mixture, which enables modern gardeners to create their own stonelike planters.*

BOTTOM RIGHT: *A stone path surrounds a knot garden planted with germander* (Teucrium) *and topiary trees.*

(continued from page 26)

fountains, and gravel paths, but other, more elaborate, stone features as well.

Geometric flower beds bordered by clipped hedges were filled with colored gravel. Stone or brick turf benches attached to walls served as wide, comfortable ledges on which garden visitors could perch to strum a lute or make a chaplet of flowers; the seats were planted in grass or aromatic herbs that released fragrances when crushed. Elaborate hexagonal tables for dining *al fresco* and sturdy round dovecotes filled with fluttering birds were also made of stone. Cut stone played a prominent role in these kinds of gardens from the earliest period, and construction techniques used for stone features in American gardens today come to us by way of medieval walled gardens.

"THIS PROUD PLEASURE IN COMPELLING NATURE"

While medieval gardens were enclosed and relatively small, the villa gardens of Renaissance Italy exploited large, complex sites to show off fine vistas over the surrounding countryside. Designers used sweeping stone terraces, marble fountains, and flights of stone steps to impose a symmetrical order on the Renaissance garden. These stone hardscapes also provided an appropriate backdrop for classical statues resurrected from the ancient ruins scattered over the Italian landscape; collections of such statues were popular garden features of the day.

Italian Renaissance gardens, and later the more elaborate baroque and rococo gardens which they influenced, also developed ingenious stone water features, including trick fountains that drenched garden visitors when secret levers were pulled and serpentine watercourses that snaked down terraces to feed pools or fountains.

Similar stone water features, combined with geometrically precise planting beds called parterres, eventually heralded the grandly formal French and Italian gardens of the seventeenth century. These gardens, typified by Louis XIV's Versailles, were designed to impose order, harmony, and proportion on the natural landscape, as though, in the garden historian Christopher Thacker's words, "the natural world of trees, stones, and water was not in itself beautiful or admirable . . . [without a] man-centered balance and symmetry." [2] Water channels wide enough for ships to sail down, rectangular reflecting pools that covered acres, and the broad processional paths called *allées* — all constructed from stone — were used to frame and define these enormous formal gardens.

The elaborate stone structures, fountains, and statues found in Renaissance gardens and the formal gardens of the seventeenth

[2]*The History of Gardens* (Berkeley: University of California Press, 1979), p. 153.

century serve as supreme examples for using massive stone constructions and sculptures in formal settings. The next great revolution in garden design developed, in part, as a reaction to their controlled lines and geometric spirit.

LETTING THE LANDSCAPE SPEAK DIRECTLY

By the eighteenth century a new romantic mood began to influence both literature and the fine arts, especially garden design. A move away from the formal garden's strict geometry toward nature's irregular curve characterizes garden design during this period. Squared-off parterres, canals, and grand *allées* softened into gently sloped hills, curving valleys, and placid lakes with wayward margins. And formal terraces bristling with statues gave way to shadowy glens that featured moss-encrusted ruins and mysterious grottos.

This revolution in taste resulted in the increased use of uncut stone in the garden. Perhaps the change can best be illustrated by following the evolution of two popular garden features using natural stone and rock — grottos and rockeries.

GROTTOS: THE SHADOWY CAVE

In prehistoric Europe and the classical world, caves and stony grottos served as homes of gods, oracles, and priests, and as places to inter the dead. Because they functioned as gateways to the underworld, grottos were associated with both death and rebirth in early western religious systems, and they were regarded as awe-inspiring and frightening features of the natural landscape. Perhaps because they seem to symbolize this landscape at its most mysterious and uncontrollable, grottos played virtually no role in Middle Eastern and medieval gardens, although Roman gardens often displayed natural or constructed grottos, complete with elaborate hydraulics.

By the fifteenth century, the grotto was becoming a prominent feature in the Italian Renaissance garden. Such grottos were usually sited at the wildest boundary of a garden and were meant to symbolize the point at which the human-centered garden gave way to the natural landscape. Typically reached through a maze of hedges, these grottos served as the mysterious, inmost heart of the garden.

The awe-inspiring atmosphere of grottos often was deliberately enhanced by the way they were decorated — the gaping mouths of sculpted monsters, for instance, served as grotto entries at the Villa Aldobrandini, a garden near Rome built in the early seventeenth century. And during this time the curious custom began of covering grotto walls with seashells, minerals, crystals, and unusual stones, turning the entire cave into shadowy, magical seascapes. Mirrors were attached to walls so that shafts of sunlight, or the flaring light of torches, would send light scintillating through the grotto's shadowy depths. Auditory effects were common, too, such as the slow drip of water trickling down moss-encrusted walls to pools hollowed in the grotto floor. These grottos of the Italian Renaissance and baroque gardens are symbols of a natural landscape which humans find mysterious, even threatening, but spiritually significant.

By the early eighteenth century grottos were losing some of their frightening associations and becoming more purely decorative. This was due partly to the contemporary taste for transforming gardens into pastoral landscapes ornamented with classical statues, temples, urns, and ruins.

In Greek and Roman mythology, grottos were the haunts of nymphs, fauns, and the more sylvan among the Olympian gods. According to classical lore Diana, goddess of mountains and the hunt, who wandered "on the shady mountainside, on the wind-lashed mountain tops, where she bends her bow of sparkling gold and lets fly her deadly arrows,"[3] often bathed in streams at the mouths of grottos. Such scenes became favorite subjects in classical painting and sculpture.

Natural grottos sporting statues of Diana and other classical figures now began to crowd European gardens, while elegant artificial grottos, constructed to look like ruins, also became popular. The practice of decorating grotto walls with stones, shells, corals, and crystals continued, with less attention paid to their mysterious qualities, and more to their purely decorative value.

This is not to say garden grottos lost all their power to inspire awe and dread, but an element of the theatrical began to appear in the ways people decorated and used them. Well into the 1780s, for instance, garden owners were paying resident "hermits" to slip through their shadowy grottos, with a suitably melancholy air, whenever visitors approached. In a similar vein, midnight inspections of the mysterious inner depths of grottos, which sometimes contained deliberately frightening and grotesque statues of monsters, also were popular entertainments of the day.

Whether artificial or natural, elaborately decorated or consciously "ruined," these grottos were designed as places of diversion and pleasure rather than as spiritually charged symbols. They ornamented gardens where the natural landscape was idealized and romanticized rather than feared.

By the end of the century there was an increasing trend toward making grottos appear more purely natural, with rough, mossy rocks and limpid pools replacing statues, hermits, and other elaborate ornamentation. Close in spirit and appearance to the true mountain cave, they served as attractive and atmospheric natural features in a garden style where nature was no longer feared, or decorated, but lovingly reflected.

[3]*New Larousse Encyclopedia of Mythology* (London: Hamlyn, 1968), p. 121.

ROCKERIES: THE MIGHTY MASS OF MOUNTAINS

This new appreciation for the natural landscape also resulted in a craze for mountains "where Nature," writes the contemporary poet Joseph Warton, "... seems to sit alone/ Majestic on a craggy throne."[4]

By the mid- to late eighteenth century, the enthusiasm for mountains had inspired the appearance in European gardens of stony outcroppings, firmly embedded in the earth, that more or less accurately replicated hillside or mountain terrain. But a kind of freestanding rockwork, artificial in appearance and purely decorative in function, had preceded the move toward natural outcroppings. This earlier tradition would continue to exert a strong influence on the design of rockeries throughout the nineteenth century.

The freestanding rockworks were in part an elaboration of the stony grottos mentioned above, and in part the result of a craze for Chinese gardens which swept Europe in the seventeenth and eighteenth centuries as a result of increased contact with the Far East.

In 1743 a Jesuit missionary to China named Jean-Denis Attiret published a description of the sumptuous Yuan Ming Yuan, or Garden of Luminous Perfection, which surrounded the Imperial Palace of the Qianlong Emperor in Beijing. Attiret's descriptions of the garden's magnificent courtyards, pavilions, and water features fired the imaginations of several generations of European gardeners.

This enthusiasm was confined for the most part to the construction of many odd, and a few very beautiful, garden buildings sporting mock "Chinese" touches; the complexities of Chinese garden design otherwise eluded most European gardeners. But Attiret's descriptions of the fantastic piles of rock mountains that filled the Emperor's pleasure grounds did lead a small number of westerners to attempt to replicate Chinese rockeries in their own gardens.

Few of these efforts survive today, but contemporary drawings suggest they were rather comically irrelevant to the surrounding landscape, sticking out like stony sore thumbs amid the lushly romantic vegetation nearby. These rock piles served a purely decorative function, and sometimes sported ferns, vines, or other atmospheric plants.

In the early nineteenth century, freestanding rockwork further evolved into a fad for replicating whole mountains. In one famous rock garden in England, at Hoole House near Chester, the Savoy mountains were represented in scrupulous scale, complete with pulverized marble standing in for snow. Another well-known garden replicated the Matterhorn and its surrounding alpine meadows, dotted with mountain goats made of tin. Other

[4]Joseph Warton, "Ode I to Fancy," in *Eighteenth-Century Poetry and Prose* (New York: Ronald Press Co., 1956), p. 564.

rockworks of the time featured embedded bricks and scarlet corals, as well as shell-lined fountains. To modern eyes such rockeries might look about as pleasingly natural as the features in some of our more exuberantly decorated theme parks, yet this tradition continued to influence many garden designers well into the nineteenth century.

By mid-century, rockery makers increasingly were attempting to combine the look of naturalistic rock outcroppings with the more artificial freestanding rockwork. This uneasy alliance tended to produce rather massive, overscale rockeries planted in gloomy conifers and shrubs.

Once the cultivation of alpines and rock plants became popular in the 1860s, rockeries gradually began to lose their purely decorative, artificial roles. Instead, efforts were made to build them as geologically accurate environments for high-country plants. As a result, more rockeries began to feature natural stone in correctly scaled, natural-appearing settings. Chapter 9 follows the rockery's continued evolution in modern gardens.

Ever since the first paradise gardens of the Middle East, cut and sculpted stone has been used to impose order, hierarchy, and symmetry on western gardens. Today "wild" stone is playing an increasingly important role. This development is due in part to our growing appreciation of the Asian tradition in using uncut stone in gardens. It is also due partly to our growing respect for the natural landscape itself — even as that landscape increasingly is threatened by waves of bug spray, acid rain, and asphalt.

Transforming the perfected paradise garden into a natural Eden means turning symmetry into harmony, hierarchy into balance, and order into "gentle chaos" (after Mirabel Osler's book, *A Gentle Plea for Chaos*). In the future, designing gardens that explore the balance between order and chaos may result in some of our more interesting new garden styles.

As in so many aspects of working with stone in the landscape, Japanese garden designers can serve as our models here. In their compositions, a natural stepping stone can erupt with fundamental force from a smooth and polished pathway of cut paving slabs and gravel, or a boulder can suddenly surge out of a flat bed of evenly sized cobbles set into mortar with the precision of eggs nestled in a carton. The tension between nature and created order is proposed, explored, and resolved, all within the same stone feature.

As Chapter 4 demonstrates, stone features can play the same crucial role in constructing traditional gardens — the new Edens — and every style of garden in between.

CHAPTER 4

USING STONE
IN TODAY'S GARDENS

THE TYPES OF GARDENS DISCUSSED in Chapter 3 belonged to the leisured classes and were were built to express their owner's power, wealth, and taste. Humbler folk cultivated gardens right outside the front door, where vegetables, flowers, shrubs, and herbs sprawled together in useful and picturesque profusion. In contrast to the elaborate statuary, fountains, grottos, and ruins found in the great gardens, the stone features in these gardens — mostly paths and walls — were built on a modest scale with simple tools and locally available materials.

Today's garden styles draw on many different gardening traditions, and they emphasize practical, comfortable designs that integrate indoor and outdoor living spaces. More people than ever garden, and they increasingly require garden styles that conserve labor, space, and water. As this chapter demonstrates, stone features that home gardeners are able to construct themselves can play key roles, not only in traditional garden styles, but also in low-maintenance gardens, small urban courtyards, xeriscapes, and wildlife-attracting gardens. Ideas for using stone features in a garden renovation also are included.

These designs are given as suggestions rather than formulas; each gardener will want to amend them as his or her individual taste and site conditions require.

Note: For gardeners with limited space, some suggestions for "Pocket Gardens" are presented. The stone features suggested for these smaller garden plans generally require less labor and expense to construct.

Construction techniques for the paths, steps, walls, terraces, ponds, and rock gardens described below are given in chapters 6 through 9.

An Herb Garden

Herb patches were the earliest gardens humans created, and many of the plants and design conventions found in modern American herb gardens first appeared in Mediterranean gardens well over four thousand years ago.

Herbs that are at once aromatic, edible, and decorative — such as rosemary, sage, bay, and coriander — originally grew wild among the stony outcroppings cascading down Mediterranean hillsides, where their roots flourished in the well-draining, alkaline soil characteristic of the region.

When early gardeners domesticated such herbs, they continued to plant them around stone features for both cultural and decorative reasons — a practice we still follow today. A raised planting bed made of rough cut stones, for instance, not only creates a warm and quick-draining bed of soil for the herbs' roots, but also acts as a visual foil to their dusty green, glaucous, and grey leaves. Similarly, a gravel path bordered in bricks or Belgian blocks (see Glossary) not only provides dry, level access to the planting beds, but also serves as an attractive backdrop for the low, spreading herbs you can plant to spill over its margins in decorative billows.

A POCKET HERB GARDEN

This small herb garden (Figure 4–1) is defined by four elaborately patterned gravel and Belgian block paths that meet in the center at a millstone made of hypertufa (see Chapter 10).

Figure 4–1. Gravel paths edged and patterned with Belgian blocks surround a hypertufa millstone in a pocket herb garden.

An Illustrated Herb Garden

In this herb garden, a terrace of formal flagstones creates the transition between the indoors and the outdoors. Dwarf fruit trees grown against a wall made of roughly cut stone mark the eastern boundary of the garden. Low stone walls on the northern and western sides are softened by shrubs, interspersed with benches. Paths made of gravel edged and crossed by Belgian blocks define the herb garden's formal area, while a rocky outcropping located at the end of the garden furthest from the house provides an informal environment for low-growing herbs that like to scramble over natural rock, such as Corsican mint *(Mentha requienii)*, golden thyme *(Thymus* x *citriodorus* 'Aureus'), and purslane *(Portulaca oleracea)*.

The site should be sunny, ideally facing southwest, and sheltered. Combinations of evergreens with sculptural qualities, such as rosemary *(Rosmarinus officinalis)*, bay *(Laurus nobilis)*, and juniper *(Juniperus communis)*, are planted in tubs and also in the beds; the stone features and evergreen plants provide visual interest in the winter.

Clay pots and stone often combine comfortably in herb gardens. Some large clay pots or strawberry jars planted in thyme, sage, chives, and marjoram can be placed around the second terrace at the bottom of the garden, which is made of "crazy paving" (see Glossary) to create visual harmony with the adjacent rockery. The second terrace also features a low stone seat surrounded by chamomile that provides a comfortable, fragrant spot from which to view the rockery.

Figure 4–2. Stone hardscapes and gravel paths define the borders in a formal herb garden.

Figure 4–3. A path of Belgian blocks and flagstones wanders through a cottage garden.

A Cottage Garden

There are few garden styles more evocative than the cottage garden. Hollyhocks and foxgloves; lilies and roses; pinks, poppies, and snapdragons: all the flowers that most stir the hearts of gardeners tumble together happily under sunny blue skies in the cottage gardens of our daydreams.

For many gardeners, these vision gardens start out at the path leading up to the cottage's front door. Usually quite straight and narrow, the paths can be made of crazy paving, cobbles set in cement, or Belgian blocks with sand swept between them, and their margins can be lost in mounds of sweet-smelling low spreaders, such as alyssum *(Lobularia maritima)*, cherry pie *(Heliotropium peruvianum)*, and garland flower *(Daphne cneorum)*, which send up puffs of fragrance as visitors brush by them.

Random stepping stones wander off the main path to lose themselves in the wide, luxuriantly planted beds on either side. Once the house is reached, two informal stone steps lead to a small porch overgrown by rambling roses. The porch, made of crazy paving, features large clay pots sitting on either side of the door, one planted with a compact evergreen shrub, such as clipped euonymus or boxwood, and the other spilling over with colorful annuals.

Figure 4–4. Lush borders spill over a graveled clearing edged with flagstones in a pocket cottage garden.

Low, dry-laid stone walls run between the garden and the street, providing a barely glimpsed but necessary hardscape for the profusion of plants growing in front of them. Some pockets of dirt have built up in crevices in the walls, providing a foothold for candytuft *(Iberis sempervirens)* and various varieties of creeping phlox, low-growing campanulas, and pinks to grow and spill over their tops and sides.

A Pocket Cottage Garden

In essence, cottage garden design calls for masses of plants tumbling over a relatively simple skeleton of hardscapes. This pocket plan calls for a square terrace of pea gravel bordered by stone pavers and then rimmed by dense plantings of annuals, perennials, herbs, ornamental vegetables, and shrubs. Evergreen shrubs, such as rosemary, junipers, or euonymus are planted at each corner of the square to provide some backbone for the beds. A stone birdbath with chives *(Allium schoenoprasum)* and white clover *(Trifolium repens)* covering its base stands in the middle of the square, inviting birds and butterflies into the cottage garden.

A Large Formal Garden

Readers with a considerable amount of land and the yen for a formal garden may want to add significant stone features to their sites. But will they have to expend large amounts of time, money, and labor in order to do so?

The construction of stone features tends to be more expensive and labor-intensive than most types of garden improvements — although such expenditures, of course, are paid back many times over by the beauty and durability stone adds to any site. But there are ways to present stone constructions in formal gardens so their impact exceeds their actual dimensions.

One way is to establish formal lines in the garden by using stone features, and then to continue and extend those lines with hedges and other plantings. The long rectangular shape of this garden (Figure 4–5) is established by stone walls on the short sides and evergreen hedges on the longer sides. Gravel *allées*, bordered on corners by clipped evergreens in painted tubs, divide the garden into symmetrical quarters of lawn. In the center, where the *allées* meet, a pergola supporting wisteria, clematis, or roses arches over a floor made of cobbles set in mortar and bordered by pavers. The same type and size of pavers are used as a base for the benches set at the ends of the shorter *allées*, against the evergreen hedges. Large pots containing mophead hydrangeas (*Hydrangea macrophylla*) may be set next to the benches.

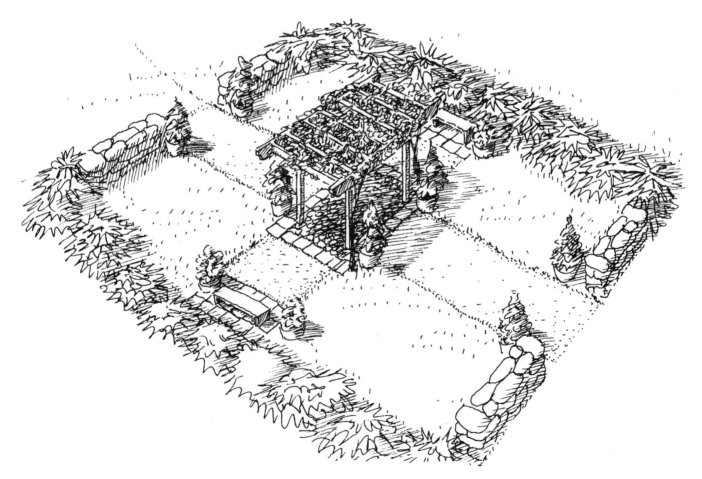

Figure 4–5. Stone walls and gravel paths establish the dominant lines in a formal garden.

A Romantic Garden

An atmosphere of seclusion and mystery transforms romantic gardens into circles of enchantment, where time seems suspended and the rest of the world feels remote. Romantic gardens cast a spell on visitors, who find it easy to imagine unicorns stepping daintily between the trees, with their twisting, pearly horns glinting in the dappled shade.

Stone can play a prominent role in such gardens, both in natural and constructed features. Mossy rocks set in small groves of trees, for instance, conjure up secret woodland clearings where travelers fall into dreamless sleep, never to wake again. Or half-tumbled stone walls covered in ferns and ivies can sink into the earth like ruins a thousand years old.

This romantic garden features half-buried stepping stones that wander between two secret glades separated by a stone wall. Each glade is surrounded by thick plantings of trees and shrubs over-

Figure 4–6. A vine-covered pergola and a stone-rimmed pond add mystery to a romantic garden.

Figure 4–7. A grotto and a small pool create a pocket romantic garden.

run by flowering vines. The sunny glade features a stone and wood pergola covered in old-fashioned climbing roses. Foxtail lilies (*Eremurus* spp.), angelica (*Angelica archangelica*), gold meadow rue *(Thalictrum speciosissimum)*, and queen-of-the-meadow *(Filipendula ulmaria)* grow in loose drifts along the path. In the shadowy glade, an overgrown pond rimmed by mossy rocks is bordered by a stone bench with a froth of sweet woodruff (*Asperula odorata*) planted near its base. Bleeding-heart (*Dicentra spectabilis*), lacy ferns such as the lady fern (*Athyrium felix-femina*), feathery goatsbeard (*Aruncus sylvester*), and snakeroot (*Cimicifuga racemosa*) are planted around the pond, among lush clumps of gunnera (*Acanthus mollis*) and white hellebore (*Veratrum viride*).

A POCKET ROMANTIC GARDEN

A miniature cave or grotto covered in moss and ferns will turn any corner of your garden into a pocket of enchantment. Simply pile rocks and stones in an arch against a natural embankment or a stone wall, cementing them together and then covering any visible cemented areas with hypertufa (see Chapter 10). Attach successive layers to the first arch to make the cave or grotto deeper. Fill some of the crevices between the stones on the outside walls of the grotto with soil in order to provide a foothold for plants.

You might consider spreading a two-inch layer of hypertufa on those walls inside the grotto which are visible to the outside, pressing into them shells, corals, and beautiful stones as decorations. Placing a small pool of water before the grotto, even a stone birdbath taken off its pedestal and half-buried in the earth, will add mysterious shadows and reflections to the site.

For That Ruined Look

In order to encourage the growth of moss and lichens on a stone wall situated in shade, use a clean paintbrush to apply dabs of a wet mixture of hypertufa (see Chapter 10). After letting the hypertufa cure for six weeks, spray it with a mixture of liquid manure and crumbled moss and lichens that originally grew on stone somewhere else. Gently sprinkle the wall with water from time to time while the plants are establishing themselves. Thereafter, send a spray of water against the wall from your watering hose during exceptionally dry periods.

A Gravel Garden

Gravel gardens hold a simple allure for busy gardeners; they require minimum effort to maintain, while offering maximum benefits as healthy environments for plants. The idea behind gravel gardening is equally simple: tear out labor-intensive lawns and flower beds, and replace them with a thick layer of gravel which acts as a mulch, weed suppressor, and water conserver.

The time you save from reduced fertilizing, spraying, mowing, thatching, watering, and weeding can be spent experimenting with the vast palette of plants that find gravel particularly congenial. Expert gravel gardeners note that almost all perennials, annuals, and shrubs flower more freely in gravel.

When you add that gravel is inexpensive, easy to install, durable, and an attractive groundcover that blends well with other garden hardscapes, then its increasing popularity is easy to understand. There are limitless ways to add gravel gardens to your property, as the following suggestions show.

Note: Once installed on a site, gravel is very difficult to remove, so plan carefully before laying it down!

If you are converting a somewhat large, informal area into a gravel garden, then slightly berm it for visual interest, run a curving, gently graded path of compacted gravel through it, sink some rocks into the gravel to resemble natural outcroppings, and spread a layer of gravel two to four inches deep in the planting areas (construction of gravel gardens is covered in Chapter 9). Rock roses *(Helianthemum)*, lady's-mantle *(Alchemilla mollis)*, lavenders, iris, mullein *(Verbascum)*, blue-eyed grass *(Sisyrinchium)*, and euphorbias thrive especially well in such environments, as do almost all kinds of ornamental herbs.

If you are converting a smaller area, and wish to keep it both level and more formal, then construct three-foot squares of gravel, bordered by treated wood, upended bricks, or Belgian blocks. Alternate them with squares of planted areas, which can be filled with some of the plants listed above, along with small evergreen shrubs for backbone.

For a small townhouse courtyard requiring maximum privacy and minimum upkeep, grow attractive, low-care evergreens such as camellias, boxwood, and hollies around the boundaries, cover the garden floor in gravel, and construct a pergola with a crazy-paving floor in the center of the site. Plant low-maintenance screening vines such as silverfleece *(Polygonum aubertii)* and the fragrant chocolate vine *(Akebia quinata)* around the pergola, and place an outdoor chair underneath it to enjoy your hot summer afternoons in leafy seclusion. Set tubs of easy-care annuals such as petunias and lobelia nearby for splashes of color. Using gravel flooring in this garden plan reduces day-to-day maintenance to watering container plants and picking off spent blooms.

A Checkerboard Garden

For those of us who like the idea of low maintenance, but can't envision a garden without soothing vistas of green sweeping across the ground, there is a way to achieve both. Using squares three feet long on a side and composed of a variety of stone materials (Figure 4–8), create a checkerboard design in a level area of the garden, preferably one that can be viewed from above. Plant the alternate squares, or combinations of two or three squares, with a single kind of evergreen groundcover for an elegant, low-key effect.

If you plant ivy or moss, mound their planting squares very gently, so the plants rise just an inch or two above the hardscape squares. (Remember, moss will need to be swept clear of garden debris occasionally, and ivy will need to be pruned back, *not sheared*, about once a year.)

Even if you choose to plant grass, it will require only half the upkeep, water, and fertilizer of a regular lawn, while conveying much the same tranquil effect. The hardscape squares in a turf checkerboard should be flat and set half an inch below the surrounding grass, so the lawn mower can roll right over them without harming the cutting blades. (In order to avoid damaging the mower, do not use gravel or roughly cut Belgian blocks in constructing these squares.)

Figure 4–8. Alternating squares of lawn and stone in a checkerboard garden.

To look their best, such gardens need trees to send sunlight dappling over the groundcover and stone features below. Select trees with attractive barks and leaves, and root systems that will not buckle pavers. Such trees for small gardens include flowering crabapples *(Malus floribunda)*, flowering dogwoods *(Cornus florida)*, eastern redbuds *(Cercis canadensis)*, Korean stewartias *(Stewartia koreana)*, and many varieties of Japanese maple *(Acer palmatum)*.

XERISCAPES

A Rock, Gravel, and Thyme Garden

Zen dry landscapes are probably the ultimate xeriscapes: their main feature are rocks and gravel that never need a drink of water from one year to the next. In traditional Japanese gardens, dry landscapes often are surrounded by whitewashed walls, which highlight the shapes and colors of the stone features in a very effective manner.

Figure 4–9. A rock, gravel, and thyme garden is drought-tolerant and blends into many garden styles.

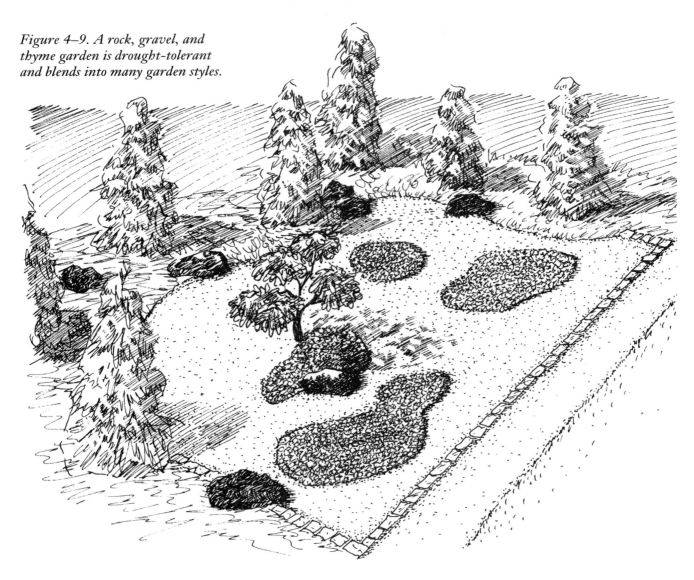

Western gardeners who would like to import some of the atmosphere and all of the water-conserving qualities of a Japanese dry landscape may wonder where they can site such a feature in their own gardens, without having to build elaborate walls around it for a suitable backdrop. They might well consider tearing out areas of their (thirsty) lawns, where those areas are bordered by relatively subdued plantings of the kinds of shrubs and trees typically found in Japanese gardens, such as azaleas, rhododendrons, camellias, and pines.

Such a garden might feature gently curving boundary lines between the shrubs and graveled area, with stones and thyme acting as a substory to the shrubs. The boundary facing the house or adjacent to a path is framed in Belgian blocks or roughly cut stones.

An island composed of a drought-tolerant shrub such as *Elaeagnus pungens*, natural stones, and thyme, softens the effect of the graveled area and ties it to the surrounding vegetation. Islands of thyme, shaped to resemble gourds, sake bottles, and round Japanese wine cups, add subtle interest to the composition. The thyme islands are raised about 1½ inches from the surface of the gravel and are contained by a boundary of ½-inch diameter dowels that stand ¾ inch above the surface of the gravel.

Note: Decomposed granite or a medium turkey grit make handsome substitutes for gravel, which some gardeners find too coarse for this kind of landscape.

A Pocket Stone and Thyme Garden

The renowned English gardener Vita Sackville-West created a unique pocket garden using stone and thyme when she constructed two rectangular planting beds the size and shape of Persian rugs and bordered them with wide paths made of flagstones.

The beds were planted in drifts of white- and purple-flowering creeping thyme *(Thymus serpyllum)*, with woolly thyme *(Thymus pseudolanuginosus)* woven in as background. In high summer the thymes' glowing blooms and dusty green leaves are set off by the formal stone pavers, and the beds indeed resemble rich and rumpled Oriental carpets thrown across a cool stone floor.

A Terrace of Cascading Blooms

A terrace of gravel, surrounded by a wide, low stone wall which also serves as a planter, can be an attractive feature in a sheltered, sunny area in the garden. Drought-tolerant sprawlers and mounders, such as thrift *(Armeria)*, prostrate baby's-breath *(Gypsophila repens* 'Rosea'), and pinks *(Dianthus)*, can be planted in the bed on top of the wall among some of the smaller flowering shrubs, such as broom *(Genista lydia)*, rock roses *(Cistus)*, and santolina *(S. virens* and *S. chamaecyparissus)*. Their blooms will cascade down the low retaining walls and sweep the gravel flooring.

For visual interest, stone pavers can be set into the gravel terrace in random patterns. To reduce glare and add a vertical accent, drought-tolerant evergreen shrubs, such as rosemary, yews, and tall junipers, can be planted directly in the gravel floor. Silver sages and lavender strewn through the gravel will release pungent scents when crushed, adding their might to a garden which is, in the most dizzying sense of the term, a sensory overload.

SMALL URBAN SPACES

A Naturalistic Urban Courtyard

This naturalistic garden scaled to a small urban lot was designed by landscape architect Iain Robertson for the courtyard of the Center for Urban Horticulture in Seattle, Washington. It features gently rounded granite boulders set among ornamental grasses, shrubs, and small trees. A gravel path swirls like a stream through the bermed planting area, creating a relaxed, flowing counterpoint to the formal lines and angles of the perimeter of the courtyard. (In an alternate arrangement, a dry stream made of rounded river pebbles could flow where the path presently runs.)

In this garden the smooth, flowing lines of the boulders echo the curving path below and the gently mounding crowns of the

Figure 4–10. Stones, trees, and grasses in a naturalistic urban courtyard.

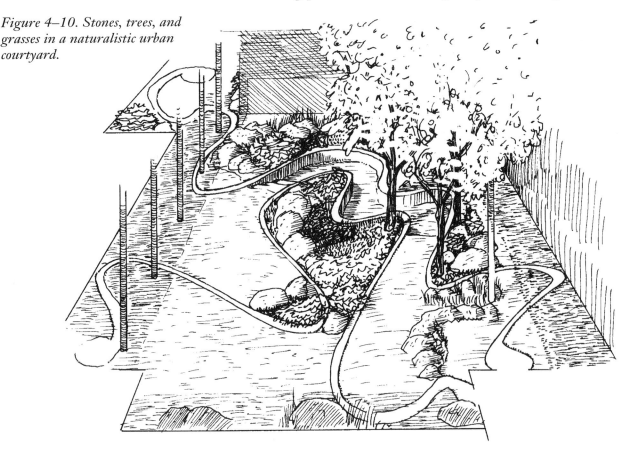

Japanese maples above. The boulder's soft grey colors set off the dusty blue-green undertones of the *Osmanthus delavayi*, the blue-grey tufts of *Koeleria glauca*, and the blood-red new growth on *Imperata cylindrica rubra*. The result is a dramatic yet serene landscape, where the boulders anchor the plants to their site while acting as sensitive backdrops for their lines, textures, and colors.

A Courtyard Pool Garden

Water reflects and redefines the lines in small formal gardens, adding depth, shadows, and light to areas which otherwise can seem oppressively two-dimensional. This garden features a pool edged in crazy paving, with honey locusts (*Gleditsia triacanthos*) trailing over the water's edge. The crazy paving, which wanders out from the edge of the pool in random patterns, acts as the courtyard's floor and also forms a bridge over the pool, while a fountain on the wall behind adds the soothing trickle of

Figure 4–11. A courtyard garden featuring a stone-edged pool and wall fountain.

water. Mosses, lawn leaf *(Dichondra carolinensis)*, or woolly thyme *(Thymus pseudolanuginosus)* creep between the paving. The visual interplay between water, creeping groundcovers, and stone concentrates attention on the garden floor, thus balancing and lightening the vertical thrust of the enclosing walls. The resulting design is fresh, uncluttered, and sophisticated.

An Urban Oasis of Ornamental Grasses

This small garden features ornamental grasses surging out of massive flagstones. Tall and medium-sized ornamental grasses such as *Miscanthus sinensis* 'Gracillimus', *Calamagrostis acutiflora stricta*, and *Pennisetum alopecuroides* act as the major plant motifs, with their supple lines and flowing patterns adding movement and spontaneity even to constricted spaces.

Such qualities are enhanced by the sharp edges and dense textures of the flagstones, rough slabs of buff-colored sandstone,

Figure 4–12. Papyrus and potted peonies edge a small pool in a pocket Chinese garden.

massive and thick, while groundcovers running along cracks soften their edges and overall appearance. Small trees with twining branch patterns and delicate leaves, such as staghorn sumacs *(Rhus typhina)* and box elders *(Acer negundo)*, act as a satisfying backdrop to both grasses and flagstones. A formal pool edged by the flagstones adds depth to the scene, with its surface reflecting both immutable stone and arching grasses to great effect.

A POCKET CHINESE COURTYARD

The Chinese term for garden, *shen shui,* literally means "piling rocks and digging ponds," underscoring the importance of both elements in Chinese gardens. This pocket garden, set in the corner of a small urban garden, contains both stones and water, set off by a cobbled mosaic floor (see Chapter 6). A tree-of-heaven *(Ailanthus altissima),* native to China, scatters light shade over the cobbles, while tufts of lilyturf *(Liriope)* spring from the base of the specimen rocks rimming the tiny pool. Ornamental pots filled with flowering peonies (traditional favorites of Chinese gardeners) provide seasonal color and foliage.

A WILDLIFE-ATTRACTING GARDEN

Today many gardeners feel that the most valuable and attractive gardens they can create are wild. Serving as sanctuaries for native wildlife and plants, such gardens permit us to act as conserving links in the great chain of being and to reaffirm our ties to the land and to our fellow creatures. If you plan to create an environment in which birds, butterflies, toads, and other wildlife will flourish right outside your windows, stone features can play attractive and useful roles in the design.

Wildlife is attracted to gardens where shelter, water, and food are available. The following stone features help to provide them:

- Holes under dry stone walls and naturalistic rockeries serve as shelters for squirrels, gophers, chipmunks, rabbits, lizards, and snakes. Build reinforced shelters under the walls or rockeries as you construct them, since animals can weaken their foundations if left to burrow the shelters by themselves.
- Natural-style ponds, rimmed with rocks and stones and at least 18 to 24 inches deep, will permit frogs, toads, snails, and crayfish to winter over snugly in their depths. If you pile rocks along the edge of a pond and allow others to trail into the water to a depth of several feet, then they will provide shelter from predators, and also serve as basking ledges for sunny afternoons. If you place larger stones with hollows further out into the pond, then they can serve as perches for birds as they drink and bathe; such isolated islands also provide cat-proof feeding areas for the birds.

- Butterflies, bees, and hummingbirds can be lured into sunny garden "meadows" filled with yarrow *(Achillea mille-folium)*, perennial asters *(Aster* spp.), foxglove *(Digitalis purpurea)*, sage *(Salvia officinalis)*, black-eyed Susan *(Rudbeckia hirta)*, phlox *(Phlox* spp.), goldenrod *(Solidago* spp.), bee balm *(Monarda didyma)*, and trumpet vine *(Campsis radicans)*. If you position rocky outcroppings in the meadow, they will serve as the "bones" for the overall composition and also provide resting spots for the wildlife. Splash clean water into the hollows and crevices of the rocks every day or two for natural-looking water basins and birdbaths.

A GARDEN RENOVATION USING STONE

If your garden's bland swaths of lawn and bleak concrete patio cry out that it's time for a thorough renovation, consider adding stone features, both for their durability and for their timeless beauty.

Landscape architect John Kenyon was once asked to renovate a typical suburban garden — a 50' x 100' lot, with a split-level house located about two-thirds of the way toward the back of the property. The owners wanted privacy and a variety of improvements, including water features, a mounded rock garden, and comfortable terraces linking living areas in the house to the back garden. Kenyon, who designs gardens in a Japanese-influenced style, first took stock of the existing site.

A slight mound of grass separated the road from the house, which featured an attached garage with a wide concrete driveway in front of it. Two paths led away from the driveway in opposite directions. One edged the front of the house, where it led to a short flight of steps terminating in a small porch and the front door. In the other direction, the path wrapped around the side of the house between two low retaining walls, ending in the backyard. The paths, steps, porch, and retaining walls were made of concrete. In the backyard, two large wooden decks entirely filled the shallow space between the house and the back fence; they were connected by a narrow corridor filled with cobbles and a few low shrubs.

The existing garden design was choppy and disconnected, boxing the garden spaces off from one another while offering little sense of privacy or enclosure to the owners in return. Kenyon decided to create a sense of flow in the garden by removing the wooden decks in the backyard, tearing out the lawn in the front yard, and then circling the house with a series of paths made from formal flagstones, natural stepping stones, and gravel, selecting the path style to harmonize with the formal and informal areas of the garden as he developed them.

In the front garden, for instance, Kenyon positioned half-buried granite boulders on the mound to create an informal "mountainscape." He then constructed a path made of granite slab stepping stones to wander through the pines, Japanese maples, and low evergreen shrubs planted near the boulders. Several basalt monoliths were positioned just below the mound's highest point, with a waterfall rushing out of their crevices to fall into a cobble-lined pool rimmed with specimen boulders and planted with creeping groundcovers. The pool is constructed just outside the living room's picture windows, and granite stepping stones connect the pond to the front porch, inviting visitors to walk around the pool whenever they enter or leave the front door. The rock garden and pool areas are both informal in style, and thus remain in harmony with the stepping stones, which are laid on a foundation of several inches of sand for stability and surrounded by decomposed granite to keep down splashing and mud in wet weather.

The plain concrete driveway in front of the garage was resurfaced with an attractive exposed aggregate finish. The concrete porch and steps, and the path leading to them from the driveway, were covered in straight-edged flagstones made from slate. The flagstones were laid on the concrete over a one-inch layer of sand and dollops of mortar spread under each flagstone's corners. The joints between each flagstone also were mortared, thus assuring firm footing and a polished look for this formal, high-traffic area of the garden.

Less formal flagstones in varying sizes were laid over the concrete path leading to the backyard, and the low retaining walls bordering the path were covered in a flat veneer of soft green slate. Low evergreen shrubs such as mountain laurel (*Kalmia latifolia*), *Skimmia japonica*, and *Viburnum burkwoodii* edge the path and walls, softening their hard edges and creating a cool green corridor running the width of the house.

The path and walls end at a short flight of flagstone steps that lead to the backyard, where one long terrace of straight-edged flagstones, connected by flights of steps at level changes, now wraps around the back of the house. Cherry trees, bamboo, azaleas, and rhododendrons are planted between the spacious terrace and the back fence to ensure seclusion. Informal granite stepping stones loop through the trees and shrubs to arrive at a specimen boulder, its center naturally hollowed by erosion, which serves as an informal water feature. Additional stepping stones lead away from the boulder to link up with the back terrace.

In this renovation, Kenyon has used stone to define different areas in the garden, with cut stone in paths, walls, and terraces predominating in the formal areas near the house. Boulders, cobbles, and natural stepping stones decorate the less formal spaces. The stone features also frame the garden's plants and water far more effectively than the concrete and lawns that were part of the original garden plan.

WHICH GARDEN STYLE IS FOR YOU?

Most of us have "hybrid" gardens — more or less orderly collections of trees, shrubs, lawn, and flowers that have something in common with many of the pure garden styles presented above, but which do not replicate any one of them in detail. While some gardeners are willing to alter their sites extensively in order to create entirely realized cottage gardens, xeriscapes, or rock gardens, others would rather integrate aspects of one, or several, garden styles they find intriguing into their presently existing gardens over a period of time.

In doing so, it's natural to mix and match garden styles. For instance, a narrow passageway along the side of the house, featuring a Japanese-influenced path of gravel and straight-edged stone slabs edged by bamboo and hostas, can lead into a low-maintenance back garden of ornamental grasses floored in gravel, with paths made of irregular stone slabs. Such a sequence combines simple, elegant stonescapes with informal, easy-care plants — and creates a harmonious marriage of Asian and western gardening styles.

Of course, what you can do with a garden also depends upon the conditions of the site. For instance, stony, hilly terrain with sandy soils will call for radically different treatment than shady forest glens with deep, moist topsoils; patient gardeners often spend several years studying the soils, weather patterns, and light exposures of their sites before making significant changes. They also assess how the changes will affect the garden's microclimates: pulling down a gloomy old conifer may do wonders in opening up a previously blocked view, for instance, but many of the shade-loving plants living in its shadow may not be able to adjust to sunnier conditions.

During this process of choosing some styles, features, and plants and rejecting others, gardeners inevitably develop their own personal garden styles. This sense of style becomes so apparent over time that visitors can learn something about a gardener's personality simply by visiting his or her garden. As with any creative activity or skill, such a style develops because the gardener is willing to take risks, to learn from mistakes, and to try again.

Based upon your sympathetic knowledge of its conditions and on a series of personal decisions born of trial and error, your garden will naturally "grow" its own style over the years — one which reflects your sense of what the "perfect" garden is.

PART III

Working with Stone

The nuts and bolts of constructing stone garden features are addressed in chapters 5 through 10. Each of the projects selected for the following chapters can be built by home gardeners, using commonly available materials and tools.

Chapter 5 explains the origins of ornamental stone, suggests where and how to purchase it, and outlines which are the best kinds of stone to use for specific projects. Chapter 5 concludes with a checklist for preparing sites for construction.

Chapter 6 covers how to construct paths and steps, the circulatory system of a garden; Chapter 7 presents walls and terraces, which serve as a garden's skeleton; and the various ways stone features can contain and channel water follow in Chapter 8. Chapter 9 discusses how to construct a variety of rock gardens, and Chapter 10 features directions for making hypertufa containers, stepping stones, birdbaths, and water basins.

ON STONE AND SITES

STONE FEATURES ADD A SENSE of timeless permanence to gardens. Yet stone itself results from a process of change that begins within the earth and then continues on its surface. This process, spread out over eons, creates three different categories of stone, each of which commonly is used in the construction of garden features.

THE VARIETIES OF STONE

Igneous rock is composed of molten minerals and gases found as deep as 50 miles inside the earth's crust. Heat and pressure within the earth cause these minerals and gases to form a volatile liquid rock called *magma*. This magma either rises to the earth's surface during volcanic activity, or stops below the surface and slowly cools there. If the magma rises to the earth's surface it becomes *extrusive igneous* rock, such as lava or basalt. If the magma cools underground, it becomes an *intrusive igneous* rock, such as granite. Basalts and granites form mountains and the foundations of continents; they are dense, hard, water-resistant stones that are most often used to construct buildings and garden walls.

Sedimentary rock is made from the debris of stone that has been broken down by the action of wind, rain, rivers, glaciers, or gravity. These same forces move and resettle the debris, during which process it becomes solidified or consolidated into layers that are easy to split during quarrying. Sedimentaries, many of which originally formed the floors of oceans and seas, compose the largest category of stone found on the earth's surface and appear at their most spectacular in the cliffs, buttes, and mesas of the desert Southwest.

The two most common sedimentary rocks used in gardens are limestone and sandstone, both of which come in a variety of colors and textures, depending upon the kinds of minerals and other materials from which they are formed. Limestone and sandstone are softer than igneous rock and work well for projects where cut stone is required, such as paving for paths and terraces.

Metamorphic rocks are igneous, sedimentary, or even other metamorphic rocks that have been transformed by heat, pressure, or chemical action into another kind of stone. Under certain conditions, for example, porous limestone metamorphoses into a fine-grained, durable marble, while dense granite changes into gneiss, a coarse-textured rock that is weaker than its parent. Slate, metamorphosed from sedimentary shale, is the most common kind of metamorphic rock used in garden constructions.

More Stone Terms

Stone can be classified not only by its origin and use, but also by its appearance. The following terms refer to the way in which stone is shaped for use in construction.

Ashlar: Any kind of stone which has been cut and shaped for use in walls. Often made of limestone, sandstone, and granite.

Flagstone: Any kind of stone which has been split into a flat slab. Commonly used as paving for paths and terraces. Often made from easily split stones such as slate, limestone, and sandstone. Flagstone is cut either into straight-edged slabs or into crazy paving.

Rubble: Any kind of uncut stone used for building. Often hard igneous and metamorphic rocks are used as rubble in building walls.

Table 5–1 on the next page summarizes the characteristics of stones, available in most regions of the country, that are commonly used to construct stone garden features.

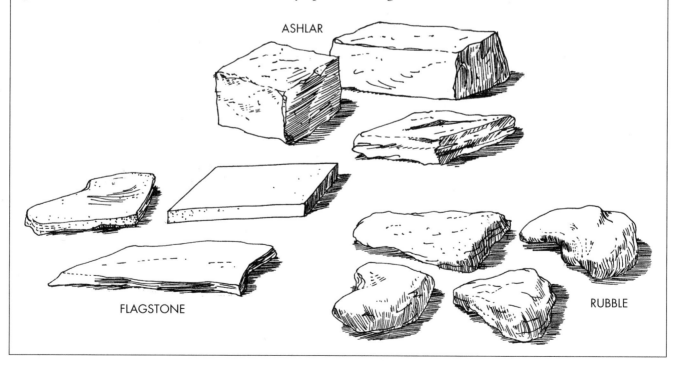

ASHLAR

FLAGSTONE

RUBBLE

Table 5–1
CHARACTERISTICS OF STONES USED IN GARDEN FEATURES

ROCK	TEXTURE	COLOR	DURABILITY	WATER ABSORPTION	SHAPE/USES
Basalt	Fine-grained	Grey, black, brown	Strong	Resistant	Usually rubble. Walls, stepping stones, natural water basins
Gneiss	Medium- to coarse-grained	Pink-grey, black, white, banded	Strong	Resistant	Usually rubble. Specimen stones, walls
Granite	Fine- to medium-coarse-grained	Pale grey, pink, red	Strong	Resistant	Rubble or ashlar. Walls, stepping stones, specimen stones
Limestone	Varies	Grey, black, white, buff	Medium-strong to very weak	Poor resistance	Usually ashlar. Walls
Marble	Fine-grained	Pink, white, black, yellow, brown	Strong	Resistant	Usually ashlar. Slabs for walls, paving
Sandstone	Varies	Buff, brown, blue, black, pink	Strong to very weak	Somewhat resistant	Rubble or ashlar. Walls, flagstones
Slate	Fine-grained	Black, green, red	Strong	Resistant	Usually ashlar. Flagstones

VISITING A STONE YARD

Of course, the appearance and uses of stone vary regionally. If you are interested in using rock native to your area for garden projects, there are several ways to learn how to identify that rock and to determine the purposes for which it is best used. One way is to visit old local stone constructions, especially National Park buildings and walls and bridges constructed along highways in the 1930s by the Civilian Conservation Corps; such projects commonly used local stone.

Another way is to visit nearby suppliers that carry stone native to your area. On a recent visit to a stone yard near my home in Seattle, for instance, I found the following kinds of local materials, along with salespeople who were able to suggest their best uses in garden projects. (As I walked around the yard, it was easy to imagine the stone-loving Du Wan, coattails looped up into his belt and small rock hammer in hand, scrambling among the mounded boulders, slabs, and cobbles.)

GRANITE

Boulders of granite, collected from the foothills on the western side of the nearby Cascade Mountains, feature slightly pocked, salt-and-pepper surfaces randomly patched by rusty orange mineral stains or dark green clumps of native mosses. Ranging in size from "one-man" rocks (rocks that can be carried by one individual) to monoliths seven feet high and as wide across, they are used as single specimens, or in a cluster of two or three, to form the focus of a garden area.

Roughly cut slabs of the same granite, six to ten inches deep and two to five feet wide, are useful as half-buried ledges in rock gardens, natural stepping stones and steps, and as informal paving for terraces and paths. Smaller cubes and rectangles, cut to form sharp edges and flat planes, are used in walls or as pavers similar to Belgian blocks for paths and terraces.

RIVER ROCK

Large river boulders from the foothills of the Cascades, their geological origins unknown, have surfaces weathered and worn smooth by the action of glaciers and running water. They are a saturated celadon green, like the silty, glacier-melt streams and rivers from which they are collected, and a spidery, cream-colored veining covers their surfaces. They are specimen rocks with lines as smooth and flowing as water, and they should be placed in special settings, such as the edges of streams and informal ponds, and in waterfalls.

BASALT

Basalt rocks, collected from the Columbia River Plateau in eastern Washington, have dense, smooth textures, and range in color from a rich cocoa with pink undertones to a warm, rusty orange stippled with gray and glossy chestnut brown; sage green and acid yellow lichens sometimes etch these rocks with delicate patterns.

Hundreds of thousands of years ago, during the process of cooling, some basalts cracked into five- or six-sided fingers that resemble softly worn-down sculpted columns. These columns, standing five to seven feet high, are used as dramatic accents in courtyard gardens and near the mouths of waterfalls. Smaller columns standing from six to eighteen inches high, with their centers eroded into gentle hollows, are used as informal water basins in Japanese style gardens, as natural birdbaths, or as waterfall lip rocks. Split basalt slabs two to five inches deep and of various lengths are used as stepping stones and crazy paving, while pieces of rubble are used in walls.

RHYOLITE

An igneous rock collected from the eastern side of the Cascades, rhyolite comes in sizes ranging from small stones to boulders weighing several tons. Featuring a sharply furrowed, flaky texture, and colored in creamy orange and rich ocher blotches striped with bands of charcoal gray, it is used for rockeries and waterfalls. Cut slabs three to four inches thick work well as stepping stones and crazy paving.

Examining the salt-and-pepper granite and celadon-green river rock collected from the western sides of the Cascade Mountains, one notices how their cool colors and smooth textures suit the pearly skies and somber green vegetation of western Washington. In contrast, the warm browns, oranges, and buffs of the stones collected from the eastern side of the state complement that area's dry, desertlike landscape. Yet another example of nature's perfect taste, demonstrated in the distribution of rock color and texture over very different kinds of terrains.

Other regions of the country possess a comparably rich variety of local stone; in the process of learning what it looks like and how it can be used, there is a real opportunity for gardeners to learn more about the geological history and the natural landscape of their area as well. (Colleges or universities sometimes offer extension courses on local historical geology.)

In addition to stone native to the area, a well-stocked stone yard will carry a variety of "exotics," such as:

- Flagstones made of Pennsylvania bluestone, whose dense, matte texture resists water absorption better than most other kinds of sandstone.
- Crazy paving made from Rocky Mountain slate, with a mottled gray, green, and ochre patina and a layered, flaky texture.
- Massive buff limestone slabs from the Kansas plains for informal paving, pleasingly pocked and hollowed.
- Fieldstone from Vermont, in flaky layers of pearl to charcoal grey scalloped with lichens, split into thin blocks for building dry stone walls.
- Giant cobbles from the Salmon River in Idaho, their textures dense and smooth and their pink, plum, and cream surfaces stippled with phosphorescent pinpoints.

Visiting stone yards will acquaint you with the variety of stones available for garden construction and give you a sense of the best purposes for which different kinds of stone can be used. In Japan rock nurseries are almost as common as plant nurseries, and in addition to boulders, flagstones, rocks, and cobbles, they carry choice selections of stone water basins, lanterns, and sculptures. With the growing interest in using stone in American gardens, perhaps we can look forward to the development of such nurseries on our shores in the future.

If you plan to use native stone, there are a number of sources from which you can collect it, including abandoned quarries, the edges of lakes and rivers, unused mines, and construction sites where stone has been cleared and dumped. Many sites require that you seek permission before removing stone.

If you decide to buy natives or exotics from a dealer, look in the Yellow Pages under titles such as Quarries, Landscaping Supplies, Rock, and Stone — Natural. Visit several suppliers and compare prices; since transport is a significant factor in the cost of stone, picking it up yourself may be an attractive option. If you plan to pick up the stone yourself, be sure to use a truck rated for the weight of the load. Check with your supplier for the approximate weight.

Once you have decided which kinds of stones to order and their quantities (formulas for estimating quantities are given with specific projects in chapters 6 through 9), there are several steps to take before actual delivery.

Most rock suppliers charge a minimum delivery fee, so consider purchasing and taking delivery on all the types of stone you plan to use — boulders, stepping stones, flagstones, cobbles — at the same time. It's important to mark the places where you want the different kinds of stone to finally rest in the garden — having the delivery people deposit the stone as close as possible to these spots may save you from hours of toil later on. If you dig the holes for your specimen rocks beforehand, the delivery people may be able to pop them right into place for you.

If placing stone in specific areas involves extra work such as backfilling, mounding, and sloping, your supplier probably will charge extra placement fees in addition to the basic delivery fee. (The extra placement charge is usually well worth it when you consider how efficiently their equipment can move around earth and heavy stones!) Many suppliers will do on-site consultations to give you an accurate estimate for the cost of placing rock. Be sure to be at home at time of delivery to ensure that the stones and other materials are placed correctly.

If you plan to move rocks yourself, wear stout boots, heavy gloves, and protective clothing, and use the back-saving moving techniques illustrated in Figure 5–1 (next page). For large rocks, a bobcat loader with a wide front bucket, which can be rented by the day, carries weights of up to 1,200 pounds.

Over time, erosion transforms igneous, sedimentary, and metamorphic rocks into such materials as cobbles, drain rock, gravels, and sand — all of which also are classified as stone.

Figure 5–1. Ways to move rock by hand.

Table 5–2 below describes different grades of gravel and for what purposes they are best used in garden hardscapes.

Gravel and small stones comprise, as a group, one of the most important categories of material used in gardening with stone. From a purely utilitarian point of view, they are the backbone of most of the projects discussed in later chapters. Different sizes and varieties of crushed rock form the foundations beneath paths, steps, terraces, and walls. Small natural gravels can help provide quick drainage in rock gardens and troughs. Larger smooth cobbles form the dry streambeds that channel water through problem areas during heavy rains.

Gravels and small stones also have important decorative uses. Fine gravel can quickly and inexpensively turn an unsightly, traffic-worn corridor into a durable and attractive path, or form the patterned floor of a Zen-style garden. Crushed, well-compacting rock can create a driveway or parking area that transitions easily and naturally to walkways bordering gardens. And, whether left loose or packed into cement, pebbles and cobbles can be used as exciting visual accents in paths, terraces, or pocket areas near shrubs and trees.

Because there are many varieties and uses of gravel, it may seem a complex chore at first glance to find the right one for your specific project. And terminology for the various grades of gravel is not always standard among suppliers, which can add to the initial confusion. As in many areas, however, a surprisingly small amount of basic information will ensure that you get exactly what you want for each application. In the case of gravel and small stones, you need to know: 1) how they got their shape, and 2) their size.

Table 5–2
CHARACTERISTICS OF GRAVELS, CRUSHED ROCK, AND ROUNDED STONES

MATERIAL	SHAPE/SIZE	COLOR	USES
Decomposed granite	Granular; fine to coarse particles	Grey, tan, brown	Paths, driveways, terraces, Japanese dry landscapes
Pea gravel	Rounded; ¼" to 1½"	Tan, grey	Children's play areas, surface in gravel gardens, paths
⅝" minus gravel (contains binders for packing down)	Sharp-edged; ⅝" and smaller	Grey	Paths, driveways, terraces
Crushed rock	Sharp-edged; ¼" to 2"	Grey	Foundations, streambeds
Drain rock	Rounded; ⅞" and larger	Grey	Decorative drainage material, streambeds, edging for ponds
Cobbles	Rounded; 2" and larger	Grey, tan	Paths, terraces, decorative drainage material

Gravels and small stones are shaped in one of the two following ways:

- they are mechanically crushed from larger rocks, or
- they are tumbled smooth over eons by fast-moving water and deposited naturally in layers or pockets.

In either case they are also sized — sorted into categories based on the diameter of the finished pieces. Standard sizes vary from ¼ inch to more than 2 inches. If you know whether you want rounded or angular pieces, and their size, you should be able to find the kind of gravel you want, no matter what your vendor calls it.

Crushed Rock

The term "crushed rock" or "crushed stone" refers to any stones of any size that have been mechanically crushed. Crushed rock, in whatever size, is characterized by sharply angled corners and many irregular flat planes. Because of its shape, it doesn't roll or scatter as easily as more rounded stones, and the pieces tend to pack together and compress fairly well. For these reasons, larger crushed rock (1½ inches and larger), well rammed into place, is often used as foundation material — sand added after ramming helps to fill the interstices between the stones to further prevent shifting.

Small crushed rock, around ⅝ inch, is usually available either washed or with *finings* (the dust from the crushing, often with clay and other natural binding agents added). When crushed rock is washed free of clay and dust, the characteristics of the individual pieces — color, shape, and texture — are more evident. The pieces will also tend to separate from each other more easily and to drain rapidly. When finings are included, the material packs more completely, individual pieces separate less, and the surface drains more slowly.

Because of its good packing characteristics, ⅝-inch crushed rock with finings (often termed ⅝ inch minus) is commonly used for areas with heavy traffic, such as car park areas, utility paths, and walkways that take a great deal of foot traffic. For paths with less traffic, or ones where you want to slow walkers down a little, small washed crushed rock provides a very satisfying combination of look and feel. The crunch underfoot and even the slight sensation of irregular surface that you can feel through light-soled shoes add interesting aural and tactile sensations to the garden experience. In general, I find paths or other walkways uncomfortable if they use crushed rock of over about an inch in diameter — but the threshold may be one of personal taste.

Crushed rock is made from a large variety of stones, each with distinctive colors and textures; in some areas, for instance, rusty red "gravels" made from crushed lava or pumice are available.

When you're considering choices, visit several specialty suppliers and garden supply stores to get a sense of what is available.

Gravel, Drain Rock, and Cobbles

The terms "gravel" and "cobbles" refer to naturally occurring stones rounded and smoothed by water action. "Pea gravel" is the smallest variety of gravel, with individual stones usually less than ¼ inch in diameter (about the size of English peas). The term "drain rock" is often applied to rounded stones ⅞ inch in diameter and larger, which are commonly used as decorative drainage material or in streams. "Cobbles" usually reach the 2- to 12-inch diameter range.

Because they are naturally rounded, these stones do not pack easily together, tend to roll, and are liable to scatter easily. Water drains through them rapidly. If you walk on these natural gravels, their shifting absorbs energy and slows down the walker. In mountainous areas, layers of rounded gravels several feet thick are used as emergency runoff areas for vehicles with brake failure. As a loaded truck plows through the gravel in the runoff, enough energy is absorbed to stop it. Because they shift so easily, natural gravels and cobbles are not recommended for foundations — their chief use is on the surface. For the same reasons, they should also be avoided as a surface in heavy-traffic areas.

The rounded water-washed look of natural gravels is very distinctive — and very different from the more angular crushed rocks. In Asian gardens they are used to form carefully patterned "seas" with striking visual effects. Attractive accents can be created by patterning sections of natural gravels or cobbles along the edge of beds or walkways. Larger cobbles, which always remind me of streambeds, are perfect for use around ponds or streams and in dry watercourses.

Note: Decomposed granite is a granular, naturally rounded gravel, ranging from bright white to pinkish grey, that may contain silvery flecks that flash in the sun. It can be used in Zen gardens, as a variation in paths or terraces composed of larger gravels, or anywhere that a fine, finished look in loose surfacing is required.

Buying Gravels and Small Stones

The best plan when you want to select gravel or crushed rock for a surface application is to look carefully at how similar materials are used by neighbors and friends, and in local parks and public gardens. When you find a treatment you like, look for gravel or stones of the same shape and size to purchase.

Like most loose building and landscaping materials, gravels and small stones are sold by the cubic yard (often simply referred to as a "yard"). Unless you have access to a truck rated for the load you need, the supplier will deliver your order, probably in a dump truck. If the vehicle can't be driven directly to the site where you want the gravel, prepare a receiving area. Wherever the load is deposited, gravel and small stone will stay there forever unless you cover the surface with a tarp; a 12' x 12' tarp is sufficient for a single yard of gravel.

Because stone features are heavy, permanent constructions, it pays to take the following steps preparatory to building them.

Drainage

Paths, terraces, walls, ponds, and rock gardens require firm, well-drained soils on which to rest. Test for poor drainage during the wettest months of the year, and then install your system in the drier months, when the soil is comparatively easy to work.

To test for poor drainage, dig a hole about three feet deep in a low spot in the garden and fill it with water from the garden hose. If the water doesn't leach away within several hours, then you will need some form of drainage before constructing stone features there. Install a system of drainpipes according to the following method:

1. Dig a trench one foot wide and about 16 to 20 inches deeper than where the foundation of the project will rest. Slope the trench down and away from the problem area to a point where the excess water can drain off into a storm outlet or a dry well.
2. Fill the bottom of the trench with an inch or two of gravel.
3. Run a PVC pipe with a four-inch diameter, and with its top and sides pierced with holes, along the bottom of the trench.
4. Fill in around the sides and top of the pipe with several inches of gravel.
5. Replace the soil to bring the trench up to grade. Tamp firmly.

If the area requiring drainage is large, you may want to install a system of smaller pipes that feed into a larger one. In this case, make the subsidiary pipes four inches in diameter and use a six-inch-wide one for the main drain. Figure 5–2 shows the pipe in the trench and the relationship between the main and subsidiary drainage pipes.

Retaining walls require special drainage techniques, which are discussed in Chapter 7.

Establishing a Firm Foundation

Properly laid foundations ensure that walls, paths, and terraces remain level, stable, and well drained. Foundations can

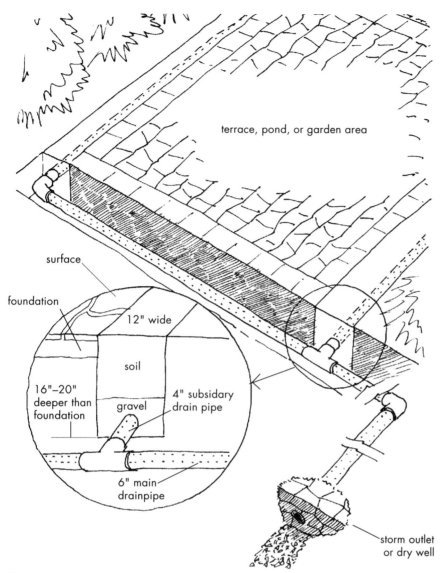

Figure 5–2. Installing drainage under stone features.

range from simple to elaborate, depending on your project and the conditions of the site.

For most areas of the country, foundations made of four inches of crushed rock topped by two inches of coarse builder's sand will be sufficient for the paths and terraces described in chapters 6 and 7, with the following site conditions:

- well-draining soils or installed drainage;
- moderate to no frost-heave damage in cold weather; or
- use of large stone slabs at least two or three inches thick.

In areas with poor drainage and/or severe frost heaves, a foundation of four inches of crushed rock topped by a three-inch-thick concrete pad may be necessary. (Consult local building codes.) Each type of wall construction requires a different foundation; Chapter 7 discusses them under the appropriate project headings.

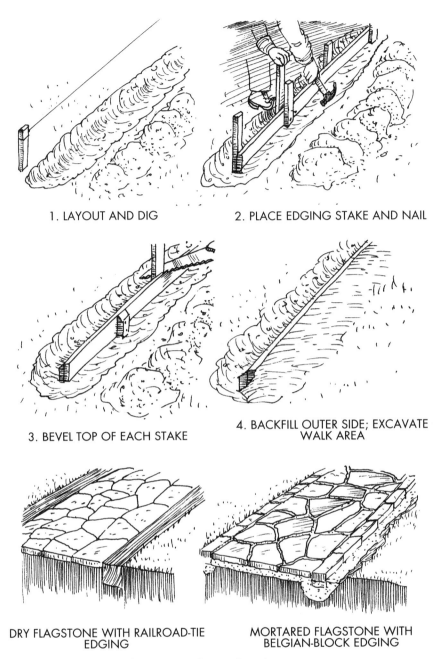

1. LAYOUT AND DIG

2. PLACE EDGING STAKE AND NAIL

3. BEVEL TOP OF EACH STAKE

4. BACKFILL OUTER SIDE; EXCAVATE WALK AREA

DRY FLAGSTONE WITH RAILROAD-TIE EDGING

MORTARED FLAGSTONE WITH BELGIAN-BLOCK EDGING

Figure 5–3. Edgings for stone and gravel paths.

Edging

Edging for paths and terraces can serve a functional role, such as keeping loose gravel contained, or a purely decorative one, such as finishing off a border in complementary textures and colors.

Attractive, sturdy edgings can be made from a variety of materials, such as:

- treated wood two-by-fours, held in place by stakes staggered on either side of the board every three feet;
- bricks on edge, set in mortar;
- railroad ties, buried almost flush with the path; or
- strips of cobblestones or Belgian blocks, set in mortar.

CHAPTER 6

PATHS AND STEPS

GARDENS ARE MEANT FOR STROLLING AND BROWSING. Wandering along woodland paths edged in ferns and wild violets, pausing in the middle of a flight of steps to admire rock plants nestled in a nearby stony outcrop, or lingering on stepping stones in a stream while watching dragonflies skim the water's surface — at such points we come closest to experiencing the real heartbeat of a garden. This gradual unfolding of a garden's features, moods, and views is made possible by the sensitive placement of paths and steps throughout the site.

PATHS

Paths perform a number of functions in gardens, besides the practical ones of ensuring that our feet stay dry and out of adjacent plantings. Perhaps their major functions are to pace how garden visitors will experience the landscapes they cross through and to point out views for which it is worth slowing down.

For example, consider what happens when visitors leave a wide gravel path lying straight across a level stretch of lawn for a narrower path of stepping stones that winds through a rockery of delicate alpines and dwarf evergreens. The changes in the path's contours, width, and walking surface subliminally encourage the visitors to slow down just at the point where they are leaving an area of sweeping views to enter a landscape designed on a relatively miniature scale — one which rewards a lingering study.

Paths also allow us to experience alterations in a garden's slopes and terrain, such as trudging up paths that wind over and down a hillside, or by picking our way over irregular stepping stones set in mounds of moss near a stream. In addition, paths and steps serve to draw visitors further into the garden, adding anticipation, even mystery, to a garden stroll by wandering out of sight down a ravine or around a bend. Finally, a well-designed web of paths can visually enrich the landscape, adding satisfying textures, shapes, and colors to the overall garden composition.

Stone is a particularly effective material to use for garden paths because it is durable, always looks natural, and achieves a variety of effects, depending on whether it is used as individual stepping stones, cobbles, paving stones, or gravel. Before discussing construction techniques for specific styles of stone paths, let's consider some general principles to keep in mind when designing paths for the garden.

Utility Paths and Viewing Paths

It's a good idea to begin by drawing your garden to approximate scale, and then sketching in a network of paths and steps laid out according to their functions. Utility paths, which are used to move wheelbarrows, garbage cans, and outdoor furniture around the garden, usually are five feet or more in width and run the shortest route between two points. If possible, utility paths should be situated along the perimeters of the site, where they make access to various garden areas easy while remaining concealed from the garden visitor's eye. For ease of maintenance and the effective movement of large, heavy objects, utility paths most often are made of concrete or sharp-edged gravels that pack down firmly (the ⅝ inch minus grade forms a particularly well-compacted surface).

Viewing paths circulate people through the garden and provide access to decorative features on the site. A garden's formal viewing paths usually are built near the house or in areas of high traffic, and often are made with straight edges, even surfaces, and dressed stones. They should be wide enough to enable two people to walk comfortably abreast — perhaps four to five feet in width.

In contrast, informal viewing paths usually connect low-traffic areas of the garden and often feature winding edges, uneven walking surfaces, and natural stepping stones. They can be quite narrow, about 18 inches to two feet wide, since they are designed to allow for the passage of only one person at a time.

Large gardens accommodate the scale of wide, formal paths more gracefully than small gardens do. But if you want to construct a formal path in a site with limited space, construct a narrow one that features a formal touch, such as dressed stones or straight edges, to create the desired mood.

Let's consider some more design suggestions for both formal and informal viewing paths:

• Give every path in the garden a definite destination, such as a view, a pond, or even a garden bench under a tree.

- Select stepping stones, cobbles, gravel, or paving stones made from local stone or from imported stone that is similar to local stone in appearance. Their colors and textures will blend most harmoniously with the surrounding environment.
- Lay out paths along strong, uncomplicated lines. In formal gardens, use straight lines and fully curved bends; in informal gardens, lay out even the narrow, wandering paths so that you can never see more than one bend ahead at a time.
- For comfortable walking and a sense of visual flow, widen paths at curves, or where they begin and end.
- Make the transitions between different styles of path gradual and harmonious. This preserves the unity of the garden's overall design, while still recognizing the "boundaries" of separate areas within the garden.

Japanese garden designers, for example, may design a path starting near the house that features formal, dressed-stone slabs, with natural stepping stones embedded in gravel randomly interspersed among the slabs. As the path approaches the less formal regions of the garden and its edges become more overgrown and informal, the ratio of slabs to stepping stones gradually reverses, and eventually the path itself tapers off into natural stepping stones interspersed with moss or other groundcovers. Thus, the appearance of the path gradually changes in response to the changing moods of the garden areas, even though the same materials are used throughout its entire length.

- Use stepping stones and slabs that are broad and spacious in design; they look less cluttered and busy than paving units that are too small. For stability and comfort, natural stepping stones should be at least 14 inches long.
- If the path is to be bordered by plants, construct it wide enough to allow for the eventual spread of the matured plants over its edges.
- If the path is to be bordered by lawns, establish a mowing strip along each edge to permit easy access and level cutting. Old, weathered bricks set on their sides work well and look nice with many types of stone paths, especially gravel and cobblestone paths.

Once you have decided where the path will run, there are several steps you need to take to ready the site. These include:

- providing needed drainage;
- laying an appropriate foundation; and
- constructing edging.

Read the section on Drainage on p. 70 if the soil around the path is soggy or unstable. Gravel and flagstone paths should have edging for stability and an attractive look; suggestions for how to edge paths are found on p. 72. Requirements for foundations vary, depending on the materials used and the conditions of the site (see below).

edge paths are found on p. 72.

LAYING OUT THE PATH

For straight paths, use stakes and string to keep the path edges even. For curving paths, use two ropes or garden hoses to outline the path's edges, measuring between them on bends to maintain the desired width. If you are constructing an informal stepping stone path, walk the run of the path at a comfortable gait, and mark where each of your footsteps falls. This process shows you where to site the stepping stones once it is time to lay them. Remember to excavate the path to a sufficient depth so that when it is completed it is level with the surrounding ground.

Gravel Paths

Gravel paths are effective in a wide variety of garden settings, including Japanese gardens, xeriscapes, and rockeries. Laid with straight edges, they have a crisp, semiformal appearance, while laid in curves they have a pleasantly casual look. Gravel is the least expensive and most available stone material for making garden paths, and the construction is easy for the home gardener to accomplish.

Gravel paths need weeding and raking to be kept looking at their best, and, if the gravel is not well compacted, it can get tracked to other parts of the garden or into the house. To keep weeds down, lay weed-proof plastic between the path foundation and the top layer of gravel. To keep the path edge looking crisp and to prevent the gravel from spreading into adjacent lawns, install an edging made of bricks set on edge or preservative-treated pliable wood strips.

Be sure to remove fallen leaves, weeds, and other garden debris promptly from gravel paths, since sodden, decomposed plant material is difficult to pick out of gravel. New gravel can be added every year or two to top off the path and improve its appearance.

ESTIMATING QUANTITIES

For a durable gravel path, lay two inches of gravel over a firm foundation (see below). Estimate the amount of gravel you need for a two-inch surface by multiplying the path's length and width. Multiply the product by .20, and then divide the resulting number by 27 to get the figure in cubic yards, which is the measure in which gravel is sold.

CONSTRUCTING THE PATH

1. Outline the proposed path on the ground, and install any necessary drainage under it, leaving the earth excavated to a depth of eight inches. Tamp the earth firmly.

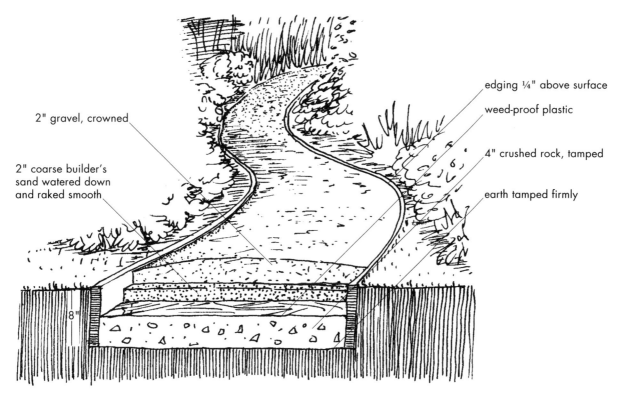

2" gravel, crowned

2" coarse builder's sand watered down and raked smooth

edging ¼" above surface

weed-proof plastic

4" crushed rock, tamped

earth tamped firmly

8"

Figure 6–1. Constructing a gravel path.

2. Lay down four inches of crushed rock for the foundation, and tamp it.
3. Install the brick or wood strip edging so it stands about ¼ inch above the adjacent ground surface.
4. Lay down the weed-proof plastic. Puncture it every foot or so to ensure drainage.
5. Add two inches of coarse builder's sand over the plastic sheet, water the sand down, and rake it smooth.
6. Top the sand with two inches of gravel, crowning it slightly to improve drainage. Use fine gravels with sharp edges in order to get a compacted path surface; use rounded gravel for a surface that will crunch attractively and slow a walker down (Figure 6–1).
7. Roll the surface of the gravel path.

Stepping Stones

Stepping stones suit Japanese-style gardens, natural gardens, informal areas, and points where you want to slow down visitors' footsteps so they can enjoy a special feature at leisure.

Stepping stone paths are easy to construct, but it takes planning and forethought to space the individual stones in the kinds of interesting, dynamic patterns that will make them attractive additions to your garden. Here are some suggestions for how to create satisfying stepping stone patterns.

Select stones that are at least three inches thick and 14 inches wide. Limestone, sandstone, and granite make good stepping stones. Each stone should be flat or slightly crowned so that water doesn't puddle on its stepping surface. If there are dips or hollows on the stone's surface, point them away from where the foot naturally falls when positioning them in the path.

When planning where to lay stepping stones in the path, consider how natural and attractive an asymmetric, rhythmic grouping of stones appears in comparison to a linear, evenly spaced arrangement.

You can achieve a natural-looking stepping stone path by:

- laying stones at their widest dimension horizontally in the path, rather than vertically (Figure 6–2);
- setting stones about four or five inches apart from one another in the pathway, while keeping the distance roughly equal between all points on adjacent stones (Figure 6–4);
- clustering stones in rhythmic patterns (Figure 6–3); and
- setting special large stones at least two feet wide at the points where paths intersect (see Figure 6–5, p. 80).

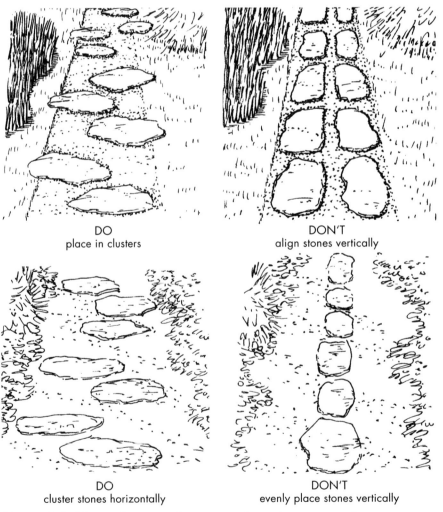

DO
place in clusters

DON'T
align stones vertically

DO
cluster stones horizontally

DON'T
evenly place stones vertically

Figure 6–2. How to lay stones in a natural stepping stone path.

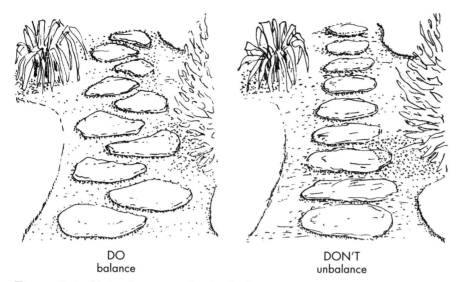

DO
balance

DON'T
unbalance

Figure 6–3. Clustering stones in rhythmic patterns.

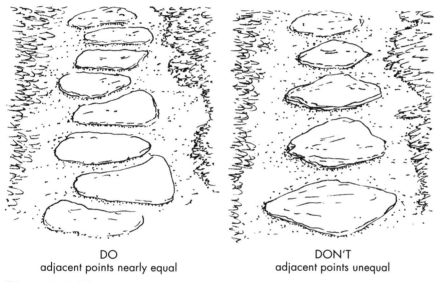

DO
adjacent points nearly equal

DON'T
adjacent points unequal

Figure 6–4. Placement and spacing of stepping stones.

CONSTRUCTING THE PATH

1. Outline the run of the path and install any needed drainage.

2. Start by laying out the larger stepping stones on the surface of the path, and then fill in the smaller stones around them. Because this is intuitive work, and you will probably change the positions of stones several times before hitting on the pattern that pleases you, avoid digging foundations until the stepping stones have been laid out in their final positions.

3. Under most conditions, one or two inches of coarse builder's sand spread over tamped earth is a sufficient foundation for stepping stones; several inches of crushed rock topped with an inch or two of sand will provide a firmer foundation where the soil of a path is clayey, soggy, or unstable.

Figure 6–5. Place special large stones where paths intersect.

4. Position the stepping stones so they are level for walking and stand one to two inches clear of the surrounding ground. (If the stepping stones are being set into a lawn, position them so their top surface remains one inch below grade in order to minimize damage to lawn mower blades.)

5. In order to look natural in the landscape, stepping stone paths generally are constructed to follow the gentle swells and dips of the terrain they cross. But in areas where you want to lay out several stepping stones so that they are level with one other, put a two-by-four topped with a carpenter's level across them and scoop away or build up the foundation underneath each stone until they are level.

6. Tamp earth firmly around the sides of the stones to eliminate any gaps showing between the stone and the earth.

USING STEPPING STONES IN COMBINATION WITH OTHER PATH MATERIALS

To finish off a stepping stone path located in a high-traffic area, pile decomposed granite or gravel around the individual stones. Using such materials around stepping stones also helps keep them free of mud and splashes.

To give a stepping stone path a formal look, edge it in straight lines made of upended bricks, treated wood strips, or Belgian blocks, and fill in the bare spaces with gravel (Figure 6–6). Stepping stones can also be used in combination with stone slabs to create subtle and elegant paths (Figure 6–7).

Figure 6–6. Stepping stones, gravel, and cut stone combined in a garden path.

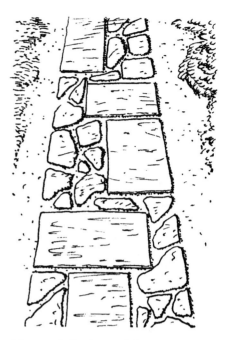

Figure 6–7. Stone slab paths.

For safety, remove sodden, slippery garden debris from stepping stones promptly; in wet or snowy weather, sprinkle sand on them to ensure firm footing. Otherwise, stepping stone paths require minimal maintenance.

Cobblestones and Belgian Blocks

Because of their relatively small sizes and rough surfaces, cobblestones and Belgian blocks can be made into visually complex and striking paths that suit a variety of garden styles (Figure 6–8). But these same characteristics mean that cobblestone or Belgian block paths can be uncomfortable to walk on, so you

Figure 6–8. Patterns for Belgian block and cobble paths.

may decide to lay such paths in low-traffic areas, or to use the cobbles and blocks along the edges of a path, with more level materials such as slabs or gravel laid in its center for easy walking. Such arrangements can be made very decorative if the varying textures, surfaces, and colors of the different stone materials are combined carefully.

The small size of cobbles and Belgian blocks also means they work well for level curving paths, but avoid using them on slopes or inclines, since their surfaces are uneven and can be slippery when wet.

Constructing a Path of Belgian Blocks

For maximum stability, Belgian blocks should be mortared onto a foundation, using the following steps:

1. Outline the run of the path and establish any necessary drainage.
2. Excavate the path area so it is seven inches deep plus the depth of the blocks to be laid. Tamp the earth firmly.
3. Lay a foundation of four inches of crushed rock topped by two inches of sand. Tamp it firmly.
4. Mix a dry mortar of four parts sand to one part cement.
5. Spread a layer of mortar about one inch deep over the sand and position the blocks in the mortar, leaving a gap of ⅓ inch to one inch between them, depending on taste. Belgian blocks set wider apart have a less formal air than ones that are set close together.
6. Lay a two-by-four with a carpenter's level on it across the path, and adjust the heights of any blocks which are too low or too high. Wash excess mortar from the blocks.
7. Let the mortar dry for at least 48 hours.
8. Brush sand into the spaces between the blocks until it stands about ¼ inch below the surface. Repeat the process several times, until the sand is firmly settled.

Laying Cobblestones

Although cobbles range in size from one inch up to ten inches, using cobbles less than four inches long ensures an easier walking surface. Laying cobbles horizontally also makes for a smoother surface, while setting them up vertically creates a stronger visual effect. Lay cobblestones in a bed of mortar, following the steps below.

Note: Keep the cobbles in a bucket of water until they are to be set in the concrete, since cobbles that are dry absorb moisture from the mortar and weaken it.

Constructing a Path of Cobblestones

1. Outline the run of the path and install any needed drainage.
2. Excavate the path eight inches deep plus the height of the cobbles to be used. Tamp firmly.

Working with Mortar

Mortar for stonework consists of one part portland cement to three parts sand to one-half part fireclay. Stir these materials together dry with a hoe until they are well mixed, and then slowly add enough clean, cool water to make a stiff paste. If you mix the mortar in a wheelbarrow, it can be moved around the construction site as needed.

Make up only enough mortar to use within an hour's time (although you can moisten the mortar with a little water if it dries out quickly in hot weather). If you use packaged mortar, make sure it contains no lime products, since they can stain stone.

Mortar needs to dry slowly in order to reach its maximum strength and durability. Cover it immediately after you have completed work — and while it is still wet — with sheets of dark plastic. Make sure the sheets admit no sunlight or air for at least 48 hours; for extra strengthening, mist the mortar several times while it cures.

As you work with the mortar, be sure to wash off any smears that cling to the stone. If dried-on smears remain after you have completed the project, scrub them off with an alkali soap, then rinse the stones thoroughly. Vinegar should remove any soap stains that remain on the stonework.

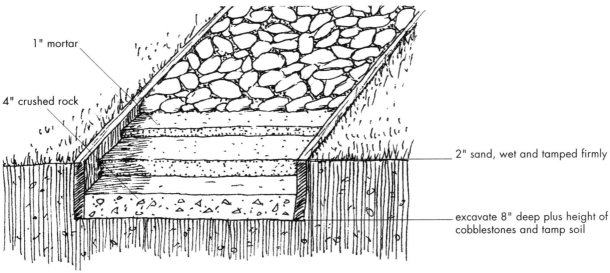

1" mortar

4" crushed rock

2" sand, wet and tamped firmly

excavate 8" deep plus height of cobblestones and tamp soil

Figure 6–9. Constructing a cobblestone path.

3. Lay a foundation of four inches of crushed rock topped by two inches of sand. Wet the foundation and tamp it firmly.
4. Spread a layer of mortar at least one inch deep over the foundation and press cobbles into it. The depth of the mortar depends on the height of the cobbles: for easy walking, cobbles should stand clear of the mortar by no more than half an inch.

Mosaic Pavements — A Chinese Variation

The Chinese make special pavements for their gardens by combining such materials as pebbles, shards of stone, broken china, and glass into striking mosaics. The construction process is precise and engrossing, in many respects resembling the piecing together of a jigsaw puzzle. The following offers one suggestion for how to construct a decorative pavement with Chinese features.

1. Outline the proposed mosaic area with stakes and strings. Install any needed drainage, leaving an excavation six inches deep plus the depth of the materials used for the mosaic patterns.
2. Install an edging of treated wood.
3. Lay four inches of crushed rock and tamp it firmly.
4. Position interlocking hexagonals made of treated wood in the crushed rock (see illustration).
5. Spread two inches of builder's sand, wet it, and tamp firmly.
6. Pack the hexagonals with pleasing patterns made from the materials listed above.

7. Sweep a mixture of sand and a little dry cement into the gaps and lightly wet down the entire pavement, washing the surface clean.

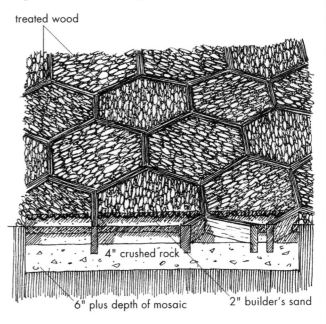

treated wood

4" crushed rock

6" plus depth of mosaic

2" builder's sand

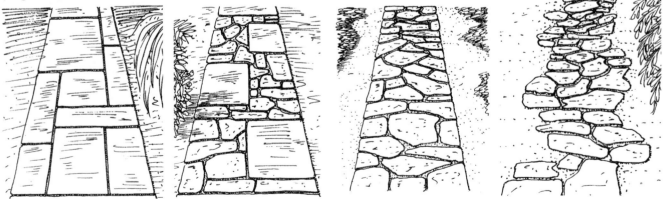

5. Check that the cobbles are level, using a two-by-four with a carpenter's level attached to it. Wash off any excess mortar.
6. Let dry for 48 hours or more.

Flagstone Paths

Flagstone paths suit formal gardens, cottage gardens, and high-traffic areas adjacent to the house and terrace. The flagstones themselves come in a wide variety of colors, sizes, and shapes, ranging from square or rectangular pavers to irregular chunks of crazy paving.

Flagstone paths are among the most expensive types of paths that can be added to a garden; they also require more intricate construction than other paving materials. Properly designed and laid, however, they will bring a sense of understated elegance to the landscape that will last for decades, while requiring very little maintenance or upkeep.

The shapes of flagstones dictate both the appearance of a path and the mood it conveys in the garden. Square or rectangular flagstones create a formal air, crazy paving evokes an informal, casual look, and a carefully designed combination of straight-edged flagstones and crazy paving can result in paths of subtle harmony and beauty. Some exceptionally attractive stone paths in each of these styles designed by the eminent Japanese landscape architect Katsuo Saito are illustrated below in Figure 6–10.

SELECTING FLAGSTONES

Choose flagstones whose colors and textures blend with the house and surrounding environment. They should be at least five inches wide, since smaller ones tend to look busy and distract the eye, and between one and two inches thick, to withstand normal garden traffic. Limestone, sandstone, and Pennsylvania bluestone are often used for flagstones because they are porous, and therefore hold up well through the expansion and contraction that occurs in cold winter climates; they also are less slick when wet than other types of stone.

Planting Stone Paving Paths

Planting small creeping plants in joints between individual units adds a charming, informal look to stone paths. Such plantings succeed best where the paths feature large stones of varying sizes laid in random patterns. Be sure to leave gaps two to six inches wide between stones, and to use a mixture of dirt and sand, instead of cement and sand, to fill the cracks. For the best results, either strew the cracks with seeds or plant them with seedlings: the smaller the plant, the better chance it has to transplant successfully.

Some gardeners feel it is best to confine the color scheme of plants planted between stones to one color and its variations, for instance, yellow, cream, and gold.

Figure 6–10. Formal and informal flagstone paths.

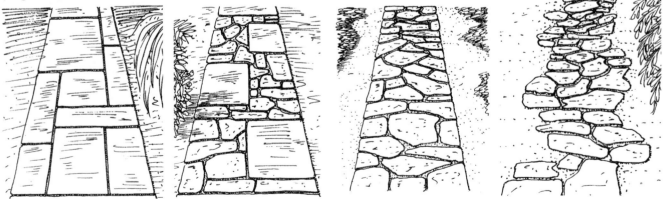

Flagstone for paths and terraces is sold by the square foot. Multiply the length of the path by its width to calculate the path's square footage.

CONSTRUCTING A STRAIGHT-EDGED FLAGSTONE PATH

Outline the run of the path and install any needed drainage. Then lay a foundation according to the following criteria:

1. If you are using flagstones larger than 16 inches on a side and at least 1½ inches thick, a foundation of four inches of crushed rock topped by two inches of sand usually is sufficient.

    a. Calculate how deep to excavate the soil by adding the thickness of the stones to the six-inch foundation.

    b. Excavate the soil to the required depth, and tamp it firmly.

    c. Lay the foundation, making it approximately one inch higher on one side of the path, so standing water will drain off the surface quickly.

    d. Position the flagstones directly on the sand, working from the sides of the path toward its center (Figure 6–11). Brush more sand between the cracks, leaving a gap ¼ inch deep from the surface.

2. If the ground is soggy or subject to frost heaving, or if the paving stones are smaller than 16 inches on a side, lay a foundation of four inches of crushed rock topped by two inches of sand, and mortar the flagstones to the foundation.

    a. Calculate how deep to excavate the soil by adding the thickness of the paving stones to the six-inch depth of the foundation, plus one inch for a layer of mortar, which is to be laid between the sand and the paving stones.

    b. Excavate to the required depth, and tamp the soil firmly.

    c. Lay the foundation, making one side an inch higher than the rest so that standing water will drain off quickly. Water the sand and tamp it firmly.

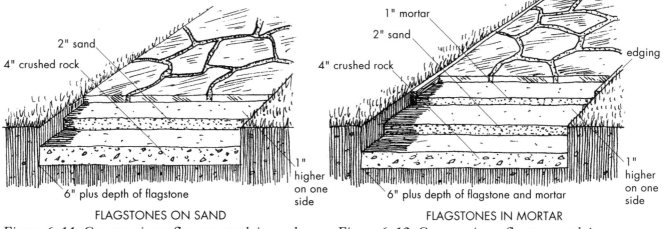

Figure 6–11. Constructing a flagstone path in sand.　　Figure 6–12. Constructing a flagstone path in mortar.

How to Cut Flagstones

Note: Always wear safety goggles to protect your eyes from flying stone chips.
1. Rest the flagstone on a flat, stable surface.
2. Mark the line to be cut with chalk or a pencil on both sides of the slab.

3. Chisel a shallow line approximately ⅛ inch deep on either side of the slab.
4. Use a heavy hammer, muffled at the point of impact, to strike along the chiseled line. Strike the line on either side of the slab.

d. Install edging (see p. 72).
e. First dry-lay the flagstones to create a pleasing pattern, working from the sides of the path towards its center.
f. After you have decided on a pattern, move the flagstones to the side. Lay dollops of mortar on top of the sand and position the flagstones back onto the mortar, leaving gaps between individual stones ¼ inch to one inch wide, depending on taste (see Figure 6–12, p. 85).
g. Brush a mixture of dry cement and sand into the gaps between the flagstones.
h. Gently hose the surface of the stones to clean them and to wash all of the cement-sand mixture down into the gaps.
i. Wait at least a week for the mixture to dry before using the path.

LAYING CRAZY PAVING PATHS

To construct paths of crazy paving, follow the steps for making straight-edged flagstone paths outlined above with the following two amendments.

1. Because crazy paving stones often come in varying thicknesses, give them a foundation of four inches of coarse builder's sand. The added depth makes it easy to adjust them for a level surface.
2. When laying crazy paving, start the largest pieces at the edges of the path, and work the smaller pieces into the center.

STEPS

Like paths, steps perform several functions in gardens. Besides permitting safe, comfortable movement up and down abrupt grades, steps can emphasize changes in the garden's levels, and also act as vantage points for interesting views of the rest of the garden. Because well-designed flights of steps have a strong visual appeal, some garden designers even think of them as outdoor sculptures for the garden.

Steps made of stone materials can run from the informal, such as random stepping stones curving up gentle inclines, to the dramatically formal, such as complex networks of flagstone steps and landings that zigzag over a steep hill.

Whatever form your stone steps take, keep the following guidelines in mind:

- If an area in the garden slopes more than one foot in every ten, consider adding steps to it. Flights of steps more than five feet high should be divided by landings.
- Think of steps as extensions or continuations of paths — make them at least as wide as the paths with which they connect, and use the same or visually compatible materials in both features. Steps leading to and from the house, or situated in high-traffic areas, should be built at least 48 inches wide.
- Garden steps usually are designed to be wide and shallow for easy walking and visual appeal. The box on page 88 gives recommended ratios between step risers and treads.
- Altering the tread and riser dimensions in the same flight of steps may confuse people and cause them to trip. Yet varying the height and placement of individual stepping stones can add a dynamic visual rhythm to a slope or hillside. When assessing which route to take on this design issue, consider whether the flight of steps is in a high-traffic area, and take into account the age and nimbleness of the people who will use the steps.

- Pitch the steps slightly forward for quick drainage of standing water.
- To deal with the erosion problems that sometimes affect earth banks adjacent to a flight of steps, consider building low retaining walls on either side of the steps. Or half-bury small boulders of the same type of stone as the steps in the adjacent banks, and plant them with groundcovers.
- If you need to be able to move wheelbarrows or heavy equipment up and down a flight of steps, install a ramp along one of its edges.

Constructing a Flight of Stepping Stones

This is the easiest way to establish a flight of steps where the informal touch is wanted.

Recommended Riser-Tread Ratios

If Riser Is	Tread Should Be
4 to 4½ inches	18 to 19 inches
5 to 5½ inches	16 to 17 inches
6 to 6½ inches	14 to 15 inches

Note: Steps that have low risers and deep treads tend to look easy and inviting, and are best suited to a gentle slope. Steps with high risers and relatively narrow treads appear more dramatic, and are best suited to steep slopes, especially if they curve and turn as they ascend.

For the formal flagstone steps discussed on page 91, consider how you want the risers and treads to meet at their outside edges. Steps where the treads overhang the risers by approximately an inch create an attractive play of light and shadow that adds to their visual appeal. Steps where the risers and treads meet each other flush look more clean-cut and solid by comparison.

4-4½" RISERS—18-19" TREADS

6-6½" RISERS—14-15" TREADS

Figure 6–13. Riser and tread ratios.

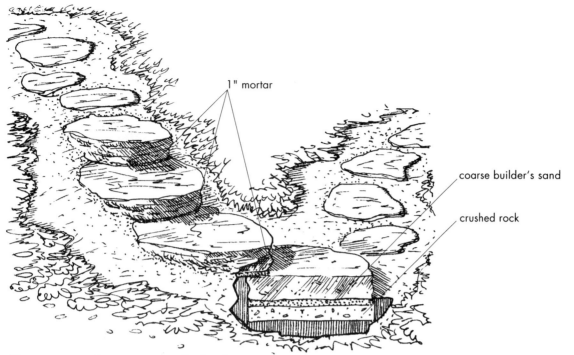

1" mortar

coarse builder's sand

crushed rock

Figure 6–14. Constructing a flight of stepping stones.

1. Take flat stepping stones at least two feet wide and six to eight inches thick (many rock supply centers carry stones shaped specifically for the task) and set them into a well-tamped base of crushed rock and coarse builder's sand.
2. For stability and ease of walking, lap each step over the one below, making sure at least 14 inches of tread remains exposed for foot placement (Figure 6–14).
3. For extra stability, stones can be set into a one-inch layer of mortar which is spread at the back of the preceding stepping stone.
4. Sprinkle the stepping stones with sand in wet or snowy conditions for safety.

Constructing Formal Garden Steps

The following kinds of steps need firm foundations and careful construction. The vertical drop of the slope on which the steps will be constructed determines their number and their riser-tread ratio, as the box on the next page explains.

Gravel Steps with Stone Risers

Gravel steps can be constructed in almost any garden area featuring broad, shallow inclines, but they suit low-maintenance gardens, rockeries, and gravel gardens particularly well. They are relatively inexpensive to construct.

Belgian blocks make handsome risers for gravel steps. Select blocks that are at least four inches thick; their height should equal

How Many Steps Does Your Slope Need?

1. Measure the slope's vertical drop with the following device, using a stake, a measuring tape, and a carpenter's level (see drawing 2, right).
2. If the vertical drop of a slope is 12 inches over a distance of four feet, for instance, then construct three steps, each of them with four-inch risers and 18-inch treads.

Note: Cutting into the slope or filling under allows you more options for the number of steps required, and their riser-tread ratio (see p. 88).

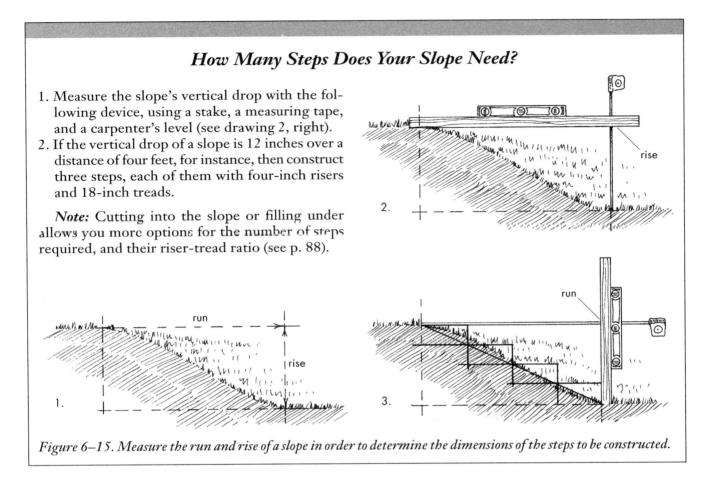

Figure 6–15. Measure the run and rise of a slope in order to determine the dimensions of the steps to be constructed.

the desired height of the risers, plus two inches to set into a foundation of concrete. (For example, if you want risers that will stand four inches high, purchase blocks that are six inches in height; if you want risers to stand six inches high, purchase blocks that are eight inches in height.) For the treads, use a sharp-edged gravel, preferably with binders, that compacts well.

CONSTRUCTING THE STEPS

1. Excavate the slope to form the rough outlines and dimensions of the steps to be constructed. Tamp the soil well.
2. Mark where the first set of risers will stand at the bottom of the slope. Excavate a trench approximately six inches deep and six inches wide.
3. Fill the bottom of the trench with about two inches of crushed rock. Spread a layer of concrete in the trench and press the Belgian blocks into it to a depth of two inches.
4. Mortar the gaps between the riser blocks, which should be set no farther than ½ inch apart from each other.
5. Continue up the slope, following the same procedure at each step.
6. Let the concrete bases and mortared blocks cure for at least a week.

7. To make the treads, excavate the area behind each set of risers to a depth of four inches.
8. Fill the excavated area with gravel, crowning it slightly to permit quick drainage. Tamp firmly.

Flagstone Steps

These steps are quite formal in appearance, suiting areas near the house or terrace best. The type of stone selected should complement the colors and textures of nearby structures; limestones and sandstones work especially well because they shape easily into flat pavers, which are convenient to work with and provide safe, level surfaces to walk on.

The following instructions are for constructing a flight of steps with four-inch-high risers and two-inch-thick treads, for a total of six-inch-high steps (Figure 6–16). The riser stones should be four inches high and at least equally thick. These steps also feature support stones at the sides, which prevent erosion of soil near the edges of the steps.

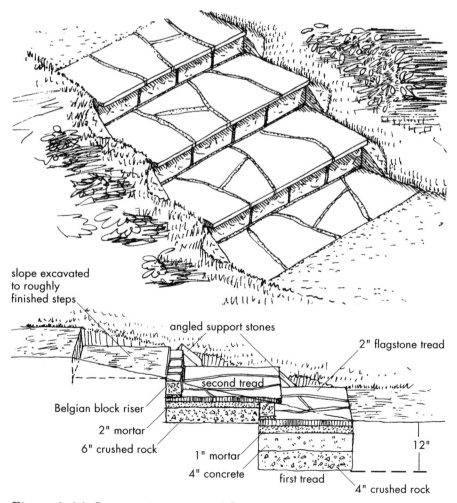

Figure 6–16. Constructing mortared flagstone steps.

1. Excavate the slope to form the rough outlines and dimensions of the steps to be constructed.
2. Mark the area where the base of the flight of steps begins and excavate under it to a depth of 12 inches. Lay four inches of crushed rock and tamp it firmly. Spread a four-inch layer of concrete over the crushed rock and let it harden. This foundation anchors the flight of steps.
3. Top the foundation with a layer of mortar that is two inches deep.
4. Also spread the mortar out to the sides, and set support stones into the wet mortar at a diagonal (Figure 6–17).
5. To fashion the first tread, press the flagstones into the mortar, making sure their tops are even with the surface of the adjacent grade. Wipe excess mortar from the flagstones.
6. Use a carpenter's level to ensure that the tread stones are level with each other (Figure 6–18). Mortar between them and let everything dry for at least three days.
7. To construct the first riser, lay mortar about an inch deep at the back of the first tread and press the riser stones into the mortar.
8. Backfill any gaps left between the riser stones and the earth foundation with tamped soil or rubble.
9. Mortar the riser stones together, using a carpenter's level sitting on a board to make sure they are level (Figure 6–19).
10. Once the riser stones have set, excavate the tread area behind them to a depth of six inches. Fill the tread area with crushed rock to within two inches of the top of the riser.
11. Lay two inches of mortar over the crushed rock and then set the treads into the mortar, positioning them so they overhang the riser beneath by approximately an inch. Check that they are level.
12. Mortar the gaps between the treads, wiping excess mortar off of the stones.
13. Continue up the slope, following the same procedures. Let the flight of steps dry for two weeks before using them.

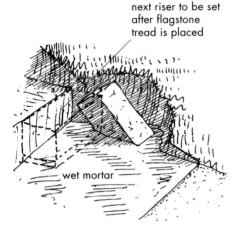

Figure 6–17. Setting stones into wet mortar at a diagonal.

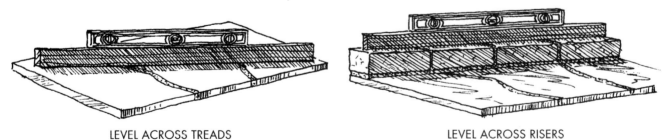

LEVEL ACROSS TREADS

LEVEL ACROSS RISERS

Figure 6–18. Mortaring and leveling treads.

Figure 6–19. Setting and leveling risers.

CHAPTER 7

WALLS AND TERRACES

WALLS MARK WHERE THE OUTSIDE WORLD ends and a garden begins. Because they enclose, protect, and seclude the created landscape from its natural counterpart, walls effectively define what a garden is, and therefore have always been considered among its most significant structures. Our English word paradise, for instance, comes from the Persian word *pairidaeza* or 'walled place' while the Saxon term *garth*, meaning 'enclosed space', is the antecedent for the modern word garden.

Terraces, too, perform a crucial function in gardens: where walls define vertical dimensions in landscapes, terraces add horizontal interest to them. Terraces also tie the garden to the house and provide level, sheltered sites that invite people to spend more time outdoors. Since walls and terraces usually are among the most visually dominant structures in a garden they should be designed for compatibility of lines, textures, and colors with the house as well as with each other.

WALLS

Well into the seventeenth century rectangular walls surrounded most western gardens, their straight, formal lines dominating the space enclosed within. Walls continue to add formal lines to many types of gardens today, from the dramatic adobe walls that surround many Southwest gardens to the rough fieldstone walls featured in traditional New England gardens. Even in sprawling cottage gardens, dry stone walls — half tumbled down and covered in plants as they may be — usually provide the structure underlying the design.

A Stone Wall Primer

Functional Terms

Free-standing walls stand alone.

Retaining walls hold earth in place vertically.

Veneer walls are walls made of concrete blocks or bricks faced in small flagstones or split stones. They can be either free-standing or retaining walls.

Materials Used

Ashlar is cut and shaped stone.

Rubble is uncut stone.

Methods of Construction

Wet walls are built with mortar.

Dry walls are built by careful fitting, without mortar.

Anatomy of a Wall

Footings are the wall's foundation.

Wythes are vertical stacks of stones one stone wide.

Courses are the horizontal layers in which stones are laid.

Stretcher stones are long stones laid parallel with the face of the wall to add stability.

Tie stones are long stones laid across the width of the wall to add lateral stability.

Weep holes are through-wall drainage holes used in retaining walls to prevent water from backing up behind the wall.

Coping is the final layer of stones that caps the wall and prevents moisture from entering the wall.

FREE-STANDING

RETAINING

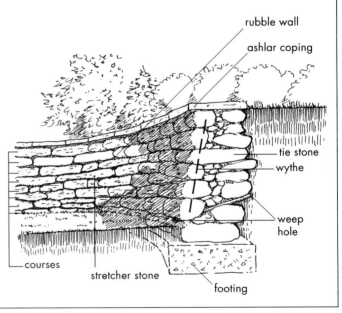

VENEER

rubble wall

ashlar coping

tie stone

wythe

weep hole

courses

stretcher stone

footing

Besides enclosing and defining garden spaces, walls serve several other functions. They provide privacy — an increasing necessity for today's smaller lots — and also shut out noise and ugly views. They give shelter from wind and weather to plants and people, and add their beauties of texture, color, and line to the overall garden design.

In addition to acting as the outside boundaries to gardens, walls often are used within them to break up the site into smaller areas or "rooms," to screen off utility areas, or to highlight special garden features. Stone walls over three feet in height should be used sparingly in smaller gardens, however, since they can end up visually overpowering the site. If taller screens are needed in a small garden, consider using evergreen hedges or the stone-and-wood or stone-and-bamboo wall shown on p. 105.

Stone walls are some of the most expensive kinds of walls to add to your property, and their construction requires a level of planning and expense that not every home gardener is willing or able to undertake. Yet no other kinds of wall lend the durability and sense of dignified permanence to a garden that stone walls do; they also provide an atmospheric link to the first walled gardens our ancestors created over three thousand years ago.

The following are some general principles to keep in mind when designing stone walls for the garden:

- Lay ashlar or rubble in regular or random courses, with or without mortar. Ashlar gives an air of formality to walls, while rubble appears more informal.
- Site walls made of ashlar and regular courses near the house and in formal areas of the garden. In such areas, the wall and its design details tend to play a visually prominent role.
- Site walls made of rubble and random courses at the farther boundaries of the garden, or where the atmosphere is more informal. In these areas, walls are more likely to act as a backdrop to plants.
- Site a wall so it faces south or west in cold climates. This will provide you with a sunny pocket for tender plants and their human counterparts. In warm climates, site the wall to provide cool shade during the hottest part of the day. One of the wall's major functions is to shelter and protect; avoid building it to face prevailing weather, which would leave the nearby plants doubly exposed to wind and frost.
- Build a low wall, suitable for sitting, 18 inches tall and 16 to 24 inches wide for a comfortable fit.
- Stone walls are more massive and visually "dense" than any other kind of wall, so it is especially important to design them in scale with the house and the size of the lot.

In large country gardens, walls can be visually softened and balanced by significant plantings of trees and shrubs. But small urban gardens will be easily overwhelmed by a stone wall, unless special design considerations are taken into account.

The presence of stone walls in small gardens can be softened by:

1. Training vines or espaliered fruit trees against them. ***Note:*** If you plan to grow vines over a stone wall, insert hooks for training wires at various joints in the wall as you are building it, while the mortar is still soft.
2. Attaching trellises or pergolas in order to achieve a three-dimensional effect. Vines climbing up these structures also will blur the wall's hard edges.
3. Siting walls where dappled shadows from nearby trees or pools of water will play across their surfaces.
4. Building them approximately 16 to 20 inches high, and constructing the rest of the wall from wood, bamboo, or evergreen shrubs, all of which convey a lighter look (see p. 105).
5. Building latticed walls (see p. 106).

Permits

Local building codes often require permits for the construction of stone walls over three feet in height, although requirements may differ for free-standing walls and retaining walls. Contact your local Building Department for further information, as regulations vary from one community to another.

Also, check your property lines before beginning construction, to make sure the wall will not encroach on the public right-of-way or a neighbor's property.

Once you have decided which kind of stone wall to construct and have acquired any necessary permits, there are several steps involved in preparing the site, including:

- estimating the required quantities of stone;
- providing drainage where needed; and
- constructing appropriate footings.

Requirements vary, depending on the type of stone wall to be constructed (see below).

Mortared Walls

Here are several suggestions to keep in mind when constructing any kind of mortared wall:

- The ratio between stone and mortar is critical to the wall's appearance: walls showing too much mortar are not as attractive as walls with relatively narrow joints. Try to construct a mortared wall so that at least four-fifths of its surface is stone rather than mortar.
- Use a mortar made of one part cement to three parts builder's sand to one-half part fireclay. Do not use any materials containing lime in the mortar, as this can cause the stones to stain. The mortar should be just wet enough

to be workable. Otherwise, follow general rules for mixing and curing outlined in Chapter 6, p. 82.

- Be sure all stones used in construction are free from dirt, sand, and vegetation. Keep them wet before use to avoid weak bonding.

All mortared walls should be supported by a concrete footing resting on a layer of crushed rock. To construct the footing:

1. Excavate a trench extending 18 inches below the frost line. Make the trench 1½ times wider than the base of the wall.
2. Lay down six inches of crushed rock, and tamp it firmly.
3. Pour a 12-inch layer of concrete on top of the crushed rock, tamping it firmly to eliminate air bubbles, and making sure it is level on top. For extra stability lay two lengths of reinforcing rod in the center of the footing. Let the footing cure for three days.

Once the footing is prepared, the following mortared walls can be built on it.

A Mortared Ashlar Wall

Cut granite and basalt, well-laid and mortared, make handsome stone walls that will last forever. But sandstone and limestone, which are easier to cut and trim than granite and basalt, are most often used to construct ashlar walls. Since limestone and, to a lesser extent, sandstone both absorb moisture and can crack in cold weather, water-sealing a wall built with them promotes durability.

ESTIMATING QUANTITIES

Ashlar is sold either by the ton or the cubic yard, with one ton covering 50 to 60 square feet of wall surface with a thickness of six inches. Add ten percent for wastage.

BUILDING THE WALL

1. Lay tie stones as wide as the wall in two inches of mortar at each end of the cured concrete footer. If the top of the concrete footer is considerably below ground grade, use brick or concrete blocks to bring the foundation up to just below the grade. Using them saves expensive stone.
2. Pound stakes in the ground at each corner of the footing and run a mason's line between them to help keep the wall aligned as it rises. Since a wall's strength and durability is severely weakened if it is not properly aligned, check often during construction to make sure the mason's line is taut
3. Start building the wall's first course by spreading a ½-inch layer of mortar on the footing. Then lay the two wythes on top of the mortar at the same time, working them from the

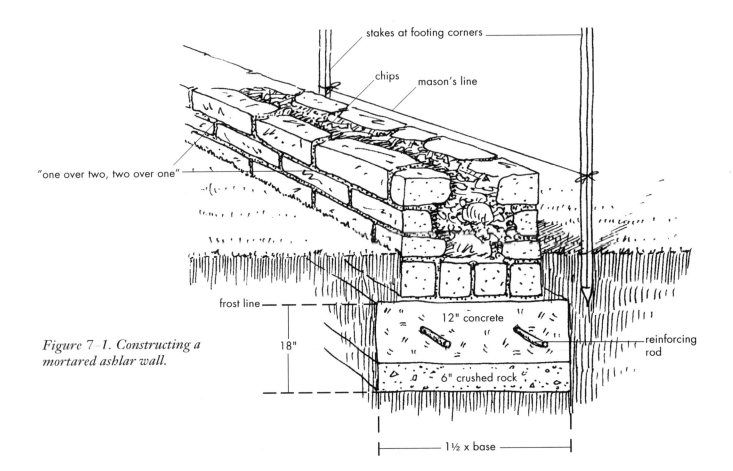

stakes at footing corners

chips

mason's line

"one over two, two over one"

frost line

18"

12" concrete

reinforcing rod

6" crushed rock

1½ x base

Figure 7–1. Constructing a mortared ashlar wall.

ends of the wall toward the middle. On wide walls, fill the cavities between the wythes with rubble and mortar shavings (Figure 7–1).

4. After the first course is laid, go back to the corners and lay more tie stones at each end for the second course.

5. Begin the second course by raising the mason's line up the stakes to keep level with the new work.

6. For a strong bond, lay the second course of stones so that their vertical joints overlap the vertical joints of the first course. Masons call this the "one over two, two over one" approach (Figure 7–1).

7. Make the joints between the stones a uniform width. If the stones are so heavy that they squeeze the mortar out of the joints, wedge small wooden pegs or stone chips in the joints until the mortar partially sets. Then remove the wedges and fill in any holes they leave with fresh mortar. Some masons recommend laying no more than two or three courses in a day to avoid this problem.

8. Once the mortar partially sets, the joints can be finished off in any of the ways illustrated in Figure 7–2; each results in a different "look" for the completed wall.

9. As you continue to work up, lay tie stones across the width of the wall about every three feet, or every third course.

10. Periodically add long stretcher stones in each course to create a firmer bond.

11. Use wide, flat stones for the coping. Mortar them together so they overhang the wall by about an inch on either side, forming a drip edge.

A Mortared Rubble Wall

Uncut stone comes in various sizes and shapes, which means that the construction of rubble walls is both painstaking and time-consuming; fitting such stones together to form a strong bond and an attractive pattern must be done with care. If built correctly, though, the resulting wall takes on an individual personality all its own.

ESTIMATING QUANTITIES

Rubble is sold either by the ton or the cubic yard, with one ton covering between 30 and 40 square feet of wall surface with a thickness of one foot of stone. Be sure to get a variety of sizes, with the largest stones up to five times bigger than the smallest ones. Use the largest stones at the base of the wall, reserving smaller ones for higher in the wall. It is best to work with stones no smaller than six inches in their biggest dimension, both for appearance sake and for strength of bond. Select the stones yourself, being sure to acquire some flat, wide ones for the coping. Add 25 percent for wastage.

BUILDING THE WALL

1. Use your largest stones for the first course. Lay two of them in two inches of mortar at either end of the cured concrete footer.
2. Place stakes at each corner of the footing and string a taut mason's line between them to help keep the wall aligned as it rises.
3. Build the two wythes at the same time, working from the ends of the wall toward the middle.
4. On wide walls, fill the cavities between the wythes with stone chips and mortar shavings.
5. Dry-lay the stones first to find the best fit before laying down mortar. Lay stones so their flattest sides face down.
6. Avoid making joints wider than two inches.
7. For strong bonding, lay stones so their vertical joints overlap in a "two over one, one over two" pattern.
8. If the stones are so heavy that they squeeze fresh mortar out of the joints, wedge small wooden pegs or stone chips in the joints until the mortar partially sets. Then remove the wedges and fill in their holes with fresh mortar.
9. As you continue to work up, lay tie stones across the width of the wall every three feet for lateral strength. On the

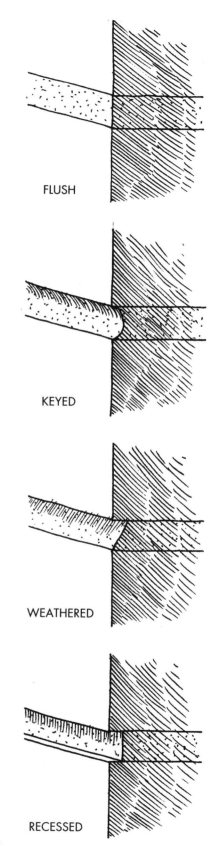

FLUSH

KEYED

WEATHERED

RECESSED

Figure 7–2. Finishing off joints in a mortared wall.

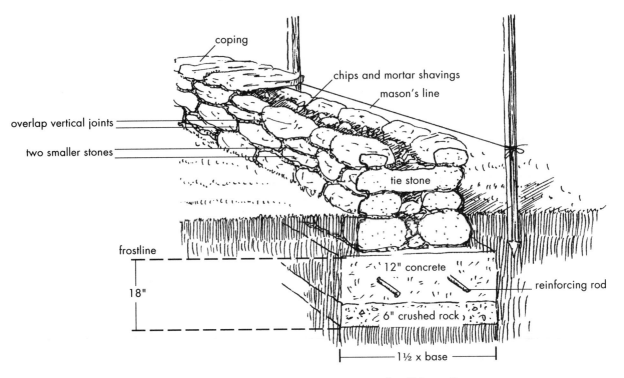

Figure 7–3. Constructing a mortared rubble wall.

horizontal surface, periodically lay two smaller stones against a larger one for extra stability (Figure 7–3).

10. Use wide, flat stones for the coping. Mortar them together so they overhang the wall by about an inch on either side, forming a drip edge.

11. Finish the joints by raking them out to a depth of ½ inch and blending them smoothly together where they run into each other.

Dry Stone Walls

Dry stone walls usually are made from roughly cut sedimentary stone, fieldstones, or river rocks — whatever native stones are found in the surrounding countryside. Because they are made with local materials, dry stone walls evoke a strong sense of place, and their informal look works especially well in country gardens.

Since dry stone walls rely entirely on gravity and the fit between stones for their stability, they are constructed differently from mortared walls.

Because their unmortared joints permit them to respond flexibly to frost heaves, dry stone walls rest directly on tamped earth below grade, instead of on concrete footers. If the wall is to be more than three feet high, its base should start two feet down, or below frost level in cold climates. Dry walls need a thicker base than mortared walls — the standard formula says to give a wall three feet in height a base 18 to 20 inches wide; for every additional six inches in wall height, make the base three inches wider.

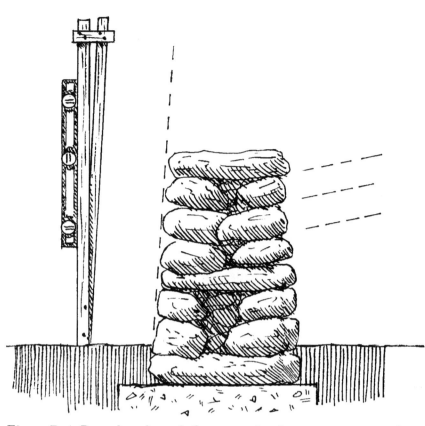

Figure 7–4. Batterboards made from scrap lumber ensure a proper slope in a dry-laid stone wall. Stones are canted inward for optimum stability.

Dry stone walls also must be *battered*, or sloped inwards so that the top of the wall is narrower than its base. Make batterboards (see Figure 7–4) to help guide the wall's alignment: a common formula calls for a ½- to 1-inch slope per foot of wall height. In addition, stones should be are canted inwards for maximum gravity pull (see Figure 7–4).

Otherwise, lay stones in two wythes, using the same techniques discussed under the sections on building ashlar and rubble walls. For strength and durability, dry stone walls require numerous tie stones and stretchers, and their inner cavities and large joints should be filled with small rubble and chinks. Coping is not necessary for a dry wall, since rainwater will leak out of the unmortared joints.

Note: Flat stones are infinitely quicker and easier to work with than rounded stones in constructing a dry wall!

Retaining Walls

Retaining walls are used where banks are steep and prone to erosion, or where a gardener wants to level out sloping terrain to make a planted garden feature. Often, a retaining wall performs both functions simultaneously.

It's good practice to construct a series of low retaining walls up a steep slope rather than building one tall retaining wall at the bottom. This spreads out the pressure of holding back masses of heavy earth among several low walls, rather than concentrating all the pressure behind one tall one. A series of low retaining walls also looks more attractive, especially when they are planted in shrubs, groundcovers, and vines. Terraced retaining walls can be either mortared or dry-laid, using either ashlar or rubble.

In order to decide how many terraced or retaining walls you need to cover a slope, follow the steps outlined in "How Many Steps Does Your Slope Need?" on p. 90. To estimate the quantities of stones needed, look under "Estimating Quantities" for either ashlar or rubble walls, above.

MORTARED RETAINING WALLS

Retaining walls that are being used to hold back heavy, wet earth require deep, wide foundations, good drainage, and a steep batter. For extra stability such walls should be mortared.

1. The foundation should be one-half to two-thirds as wide as the height of the wall, and made of poured concrete filled with reinforcing bars over crushed rock set below the frost line (see Figure 7–1 on p. 98).
2. Before building the wall, excavate an area directly behind it several inches below grade and lay a drainpipe four inches wide set in gravel to carry away excess water.
3. Lay the stones as for a mortared wall (see Figure 7–3 on p. 100), battering the walls two inches for each foot of wall height.

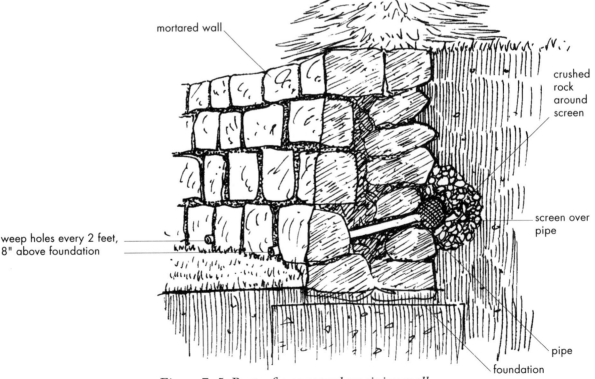

mortared wall

crushed rock around screen

weep holes every 2 feet, 8" above foundation

screen over pipe

pipe

foundation

Figure 7–5. Parts of a mortared retaining wall.

4. Install weep holes angled downward about every two feet, making sure they are eight inches from the foundation. Place a screen over the end of the weep-hole pipe embedded in the earth behind the wall and pile crushed rock around it to prevent clogging from debris (Figure 7–5). As the courses rise, continue to fill in between them and the earth bank with gravel or small stones for fast drainage.

5. Cap the wall with a coping of flat stones 12 to 18 inches wide, mortaring them to keep out moisture.

DRY RETAINING WALLS

Retaining walls that are decorative rather than functional can be built with the same foundation and stone-laying techniques as a dry wall (see p. 100), with the following changes:

1. Make the foundation one-half to two-thirds as wide as the wall is high.
2. Batter the wall two or three inches for each foot of wall height.
3. If the retaining wall is less than three feet high and adjoins a stable bank of earth, you need build it only one stone thick.

Planting a Dry Stone Wall

It's best to plant up a dry wall as you are building it, since this permits you to establish mature plants in fairly deep pockets of soil, and to water them thoroughly at the time of planting. Planting as you build also allows you to make various soil mixes for plants with different cultural requirements. A sandy, well-draining soil will suit alpine plants, sedums, and herbs, for instance, while a richer soil, amended with compost, provides just the right environment for rock ferns and dainty woodland plants.

To establish planting pockets in your dry wall, leave a gap between two adjoining stones. Fill in the gaps, and the areas behind them, with soil cushioned on all sides by coarse sphagnum moss or hay, which will keep the soil from filtering away when watered. Gently spread the roots of the wall plant in a fan shape, press them into the soil, and water the plant gently. Continue building the wall, establishing planting pockets in each course as you go.

The key to designing a dry wall planting is to make it look as natural as possible: evenly spaced planting pockets, for instance, will create an artificial effect. Instead, establish groups of the same plant in drifts over the face of the wall, as

though they were brought there naturally by wind-borne seeds or by the soft penetration of neighboring roots. Also, tie the wall to its surroundings by establishing the same combinations of plants in the wall, at its base, and in loose clumps extending out from the base.

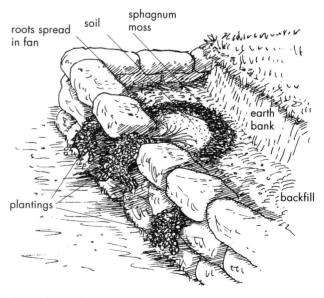

Planting a dry stone wall.

Note: It is not necessary to install weep holes or coping on dry retaining walls, since the water leaches through the stones. Do, however, fill in the area between the wall and the earth bank with coarse gravel to promote fast drainage.

Veneer Walls

Veneer stone, usually made from a stratified stone cut to a four-inch thickness, can be mortared onto existing concrete block walls as part of a garden renovation.

1. Wash down the concrete block wall and let it dry completely.
2. Excavate to the block wall's concrete footer.
3. Mix a mortar made of one part portland cement, one part fireclay, and six parts sand, and stir in enough water to make a stiff paste.
4. Spread one inch of mortar on the footer and lay the first course of veneer. Wipe off excess mortar from the veneer immediately.
5. Mortar each course to the course underneath it and to the concrete wall. Lay the veneer stones in a "two over one, one over two" pattern, so that their joints overlap (Figure 7–6).
6. Use wide, flat stones for the coping. Mortar them together so they hang over either side of the wall by about an inch, forming a drip edge.

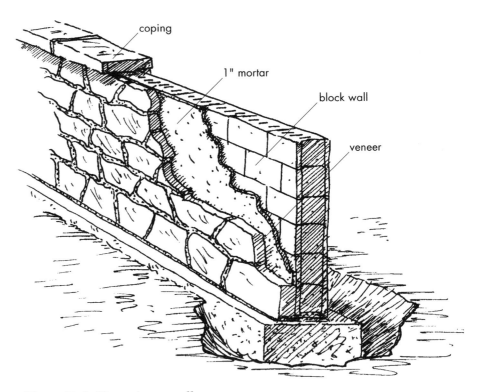

Figure 7–6. Veneering a wall.

Figure 7–7. A wall made of stone and wood.

Stone Walls Combined with Other Materials

I have seen a variety of walls made with stone, wood, and bamboo in private gardens in Hawaii and at the Japanese Garden in Washington Park in Portland, Oregon. Such walls provide attractive options for a garden spot where both the solidity of stone and the lightness of wood or bamboo are wanted in the same feature.

In the example above, a wall of stone 16 to 20 inches high acts as a base for the lighter fence material rising approximately five feet on top of the wall. The wood posts or bamboo poles are mortared into the wall for extra stability. Continue with alternate courses of squared and long, flat stones (Figure 7–7).

Figure 7–8. A latticed wall (see p. 106).

Latticed Walls

Latticed stone walls allow breezes and sunlight to enter a garden, and seem less visually dense than a solid stone wall. The openings can be in a regular or random pattern, depending on taste. To build a latticed wall, use the same construction techniques as for other stone walls, but use a mix of long, flat stones and stones that are roughly squared. First, construct a course of squared stones, with spaces left wherever you wish to have wall openings. Top it with a second course made of the long, flat stones. Make sure the long, flat stones join over the middle of a square stone in the course below (see Figure 7–8, p. 105).

TERRACES

The hot countries of the Middle East and the Mediterranean developed terraces as outdoor living areas immediately adjacent to the house, where cooling fountains, leafy vine canopies, and decorated floors and walls made the transition point between indoors and outdoors especially comfortable and welcoming.

Terraces serve the same basic function today. Because we use them to entertain, for dining, and as viewing points from which to contemplate the garden, they are among the most important living areas in a house during warm weather. For apartment and townhouse dwellers, terraces may represent their major point of access to private outdoor space. On larger properties, terraces can be built wherever an outdoor spot for rest and repose is wanted: a secret enclosure at the end of a woodland path, a sheltered area for sunning, or a dry, level viewing point near a pond.

Wherever they are located, and whatever functions they serve, terraces should always seem settled into a site, rather than imposed upon it, and their materials should blend in with the surrounding plants and buildings.

When deciding where to build a terrace and what its dimensions should be, keep the following suggestions in mind:

- Terraces need a generous horizontal sweep, especially ones adjacent to a building: a narrow strip tacked onto the back of a house is neither inviting nor functional. A standard rule of thumb suggests making a terrace at least two-thirds as wide as the house is tall, as measured up to the eaves.
- If you want to terrace a large area for family activities and entertaining, but feel that the resulting construction would look too massive for the rest of the site, consider building several smaller terraces that are linked by paths, steps, and plants. (See "A Belgian Block Terrace," p. 110.)
- Orient terraces so that they will make for comfortable outside living for as many months of the year as possible. In hot climates, for example, site the terrace where it will

catch cooling breezes and the shade, or consider building pergolas and overhead canopies on a terrace that is exposed to the sun during the hot hours of the day. This is especially important when the floor of a terrace is made of stone, which tends to build up heat and to retain it for hours.

In a cold climate, site the terrace where it will receive maximum sun, and consider enclosing it partially, perhaps with a southwest-facing wall that will absorb and radiate heat. Adding a sheltered fireplace to such a terrace means it can be used in regions where summer evenings are chilly.

An east-facing terrace will be a marvelous setting for eating breakfast and watching children play during the early part of the day, but if you plan to use your terrace mainly for evening entertaining, a west-facing terrace will catch the last rays of the sun.

- If your house is on a slope, site terraces where they will not only visually tie the building and terrain together but also provide level, comfortable transitions between the indoors and the outdoors.

Pergolas

Pergolas add a settled, stately look to a garden, and are particularly well suited to act as focal points over a broad path, or as vine-bearing canopies for a terrace. Making pergolas involves using techniques borrowed from several earlier projects.

1. Construct a concrete footer as for a mortared wall (see p. 97). Insert steel rods in the footer.
2. Build up a wall of concrete blocks, using the steel rods as its inner core.

3. Fill the inner cavity with poured concrete.
4. Use veneer (see p. 104) to dress the concrete-block wall.
5. Mortar peeler poles or 6x4s onto the top of the pergola and then add crosspieces.

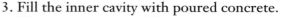

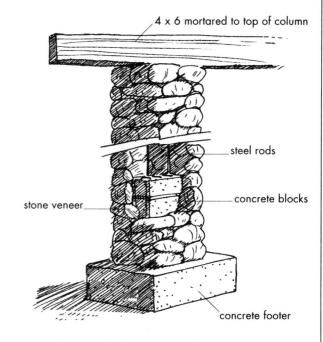

A pergola adds definition to a garden space and provides support for vines.

Construction detail of a pergola pillar.

- Access to a terrace, especially one attached to a house, should feel easy and inviting. Build broad paths and steps near the terrace, and make doorways between the house and terrace wide and level.

Once you have decided on the dimensions and siting of a terrace, its design and materials are your next considerations. It may be useful here to distinguish between terraces with views and those that are enclosed or have no view. If you are designing a view terrace, focus attention out toward the view rather than onto the terrace itself by using clean, uncluttered, and nondistracting flooring materials, such as formal flagstones or gravel. Several large and dramatic groupings of potted plants suits this kind of terrace better than a litter of small pots scattered individually around the terrace.

The more intimate atmosphere of an enclosed terrace or of one with no view requires a more detailed attention to surfaces and decorations. In the Middle East and the Mediterranean, such terraces traditionally are decorated with pools, fountains, statues, painted tiles, wall murals, and pots of rare and beautiful plants. Stone floors with rich textures and intricate designs, such as interlocking pavers of varying sizes or cobbles and pebbles set in patterns, also can play a role in decorating them. (See the illustration on p. 83 for pebble mosaics.)

Once you have decided where to construct the terrace and what materials to use, there are several steps involved in preparing the site, including:

- installing needed drainage;
- constructing edgings; and
- laying an appropriate foundation.

Read the section on Drainage in Chapter 5 (p. 70) if the soil around the terrace is unstable or soggy. Terraces need edging for appearance and durability; suggestions for edging them can be found on p. 72. Requirements for foundations vary, depending on the materials used and the site conditions.

A Gravel Terrace

Gravel terraces are easy and inexpensive to build, and their informal looks suit gravel gardens and areas near rockeries especially well. Gravel terraces are less desirable when adjoining houses, since shoes often track gravel into the house and garden furniture tends to wobble on the unstable surface. Also, their sharp and compacted surfaces are uncomfortable for children to play on (although a deep layer of rounded pea gravel makes a good flooring for a children's play area). To maintain their crisp, clean looks, such terraces require regular raking and leveling.

Using several different sizes and colors of gravel on a terrace adds contrast and visual interest. Edging a gravel terrace in bricks, Belgian blocks, or straight-edged flagstones gives it a more for-

Figure 7–9. Cut stone slabs in a gravel terrace.

mal appearance and ties it visually to nearby structures made of the same materials. Adding slabs of cut stone or stepping stones to gravel flooring also gives it a visual dynamism (Figure 7–9).

Estimating Quantities

For a durable gravel terrace, lay two inches of gravel over a firm foundation (see below). Estimate the amount of gravel you will need by multiplying the length of the terrace by its width. Multiply the product by .20, and then divide the resulting number by 27 to get the figure in cubic yards, which is the measure in which gravel is sold.

Constructing a Gravel Terrace

1. Outline the proposed terrace area with stakes and strings. Install any necessary drainage (see p. 70), leaving an excavation eight inches deep. Grade the excavation. If the terrace adjoins the house, slope the grade away from the house about ¼ inch per foot for drainage. Tamp the earth firmly.
2. Construct the edging.

3. Lay down four inches of crushed rock for the foundation and tamp it.
4. Lay down sheets of weedproof plastic, puncturing them every foot or so to provide drainage.
5. Spread two inches of coarse builder's sand over the plastic and level it.
6. Top the sand with one inch of gravel and tamp it firmly. Then spread the second, final layer one inch deep and tamp it firmly.

A Belgian Block Terrace

Curving and circular terraces made from Belgian blocks can add visual energy and interest to an otherwise dull garden area (Figure 7–10). Linking several of these terraces also creates visual harmony in a small garden area where more than one terrace is within view at a time. Belgian blocks also can be combined in pleasing patterns with brick and other kinds of stone, such as gravel, flagstones, and cobbles (Figure 7–11).

Belgian blocks are somewhat uncomfortable to walk on and provide an unstable support for garden furniture, although mortaring them to a foundation ensures a more stable surface.

Figure 7–10. A circular terrace of Belgian blocks.

| BLOCK AND BRICK | BLOCK AND FLAGSTONE |

| BLOCK AND GRAVEL | BLOCK AND COBBLESTONE |

Figure 7–11. Combining Belgian blocks, flagstones, cobbles, and gravel in terraces.

ESTIMATING QUANTITIES

Belgian blocks are ordered according to the square footage to be covered. To calculate the square footage of a circular terrace, measure its radius, square that number, and multiply the resulting figure by 3.14.

CONSTRUCTING A BELGIAN BLOCK TERRACE

1. Outline the proposed terrace area with ropes or garden hoses, making sure the radius is even at all points on the circumference of the circle.
2. Install any needed drainage, leaving an excavation seven inches deep plus the depth of the blocks to be laid. Tamp the earth firmly.
3. Grade the excavation. If the terrace adjoins the house, slope the grade away from the house about ¼ inch per foot for drainage.
4. Lay a foundation of four inches of crushed rock, topped by two inches of sand. Wet the foundation and tamp it firmly.
5. Spread a layer of the mortar about one inch deep over the sand (see "Working with Mortar," p. 82). Position the

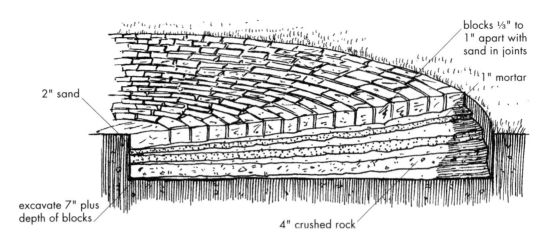

Figure 7–12. Constructing a mortared terrace with Belgian blocks.

blocks in the mortar, starting at the center of the circle and working outward in a spiral toward the circumference. Leave a gap of ⅓ to 1 inch between the blocks, depending on taste. Closely packed blocks will provide the most solid surface for shoes and outdoor furniture.

6. Lay a board with a carpenter's level on it across the completed work, adjusting the heights of any blocks that are too high or too low. Wash any excess mortar from the blocks.

7. Let the mortar dry for 48 hours.

8. Brush sand into the gaps between the blocks until it stands ¼ inch below grade. Repeat the process several times, until the sand has firmly settled.

Mortared Flagstone Terraces

Because of their formal appearance, mortared flagstone terraces are particularly well situated next to the house; their smooth surfaces also provide a stable floor for outdoor furniture. Purchase flagstones between one and two inches thick for normal garden traffic, and mortar them to a foundation for stability and durability. Limestone, sandstone, and slate make durable and attractive flagstones.

Crazy paving sometimes can appear busy and visually distracting, but edging it with straight-edged paving units such as bricks, Belgian blocks, and square or rectangular flagstones can quiet it down effectively. Refer to "How to Cut Flagstones" on p. 86 if you are working with flagstones that need to be reshaped to an area or to a pattern.

ESTIMATING QUANTITIES

Flagstone for terraces is sold by the square foot. Multiply the length of the terrace by its width to calculate the square footage. Add ten percent wastage for straight-edged flagstones and 25 percent wastage for crazy paving.

1. Outline the proposed terrace area with stakes and string. Install any needed drainage, leaving an excavation six inches deep, plus the depth of the flagstone to be laid. If you are using crazy paving of varying thicknesses, make the layer of sand four inches deep for easier leveling.
2. Grade the excavation, sloping it away from the adjoining house about ⅛ inch per foot for drainage. Tamp the soil firmly.
3. Lay four inches of crushed rock and spread two inches of builder's sand over it. Wet the foundation and tamp it firmly.
4. Install edgings.
5. Dry-lay the flagstones first, trying for a pleasing pattern. Work from the edges of the terrace toward the center.
6. After you have decided on a pattern, move the flagstones to the side. Lay dollops of mortar on top of the sand and position the flagstones back onto the mortar, leaving gaps between individual stones ¼ to 1 inch wide, depending on taste.
7. Brush a mixture of dry cement and sand into the gaps between the flagstones.
8. Gently hose the surface of the flagstones to clean them of excess mortar.
9. Let the terrace cure for at least a week before use.

Figure 7–13. Dry flagstones set into a groundcover or lawn (see p. 114).

Dry Flagstones Set into Lawns or Groundcovers

Flagstones at least 16 inches wide and deep and 1½ inches thick can be laid directly on a foundation of four inches of crushed rock topped with two inches of builder's sand, without any formal edging. These terraces can be made to seem unobtrusive and informal if wide gaps are left between the stones and plants are allowed to grow between them. Figure 7–13 on p. 113 shows how an elegantly understated terrace can define a garden area while at the same time blending in with its surroundings. The larger flagstones carry through the momentum of the paths leading to the terrace.

A Japanese Touch for Stone Terraces

A combination of natural stepping stones, cut slabs, and gravel can add refined detail to small viewing areas, as shown in Figure 7–14. Prepare the foundation for this kind of terrace as for a gravel terrace (see p. 109).

Figure 7–14. A Japanese touch for a stone terrace.

CHAPTER 8

STONE WATER FEATURES

IF WALLS ENCLOSE A GARDEN, then water features open it up to the sky, to the weather, and to the surrounding landscape. A circular reflecting pond, for instance, sitting as round and still as an eye in the center of a garden, mirrors clouds or nearby treetops; later, wind and rain can ruffle or pock the same pond's surface into an everchanging series of patterns and textures.

Running water features also add sound and motion to the garden. A waterfall in full spate, a swollen stream in spring spinning cherry blossoms or willow catkins between brimming banks — each adds its own particular rush of light and "white noise" to the landscape.

The combination of water and stone in a garden creates a special magic, perhaps because each element embodies qualities — movement and rest, transparency and solidity — that are in pure opposition to one another. At the same time, water and stone play complementary roles, ones that Chinese gardeners symbolize by comparing how stone channels water (which they term *ch'i*, the condensation of life energy) to veins funneling blood through the body. In both the Asian and western traditions, the way that water, sinuous and mercurial, laps around immutable stone has proved fascinating to gardeners for thousands of years, and water-and-stone features remain today as some of the most atmospheric elements you can add to your own garden.

This chapter discusses how natural and cut stone, cobbles, and gravel can be used in the design and construction of ponds, streams, waterfalls, and fountains.

Note: Electric pumps can be used to recycle water in ponds, streams, waterfalls, and fountains. Consult your supplier for the pump with the correct capacity for your water feature.

The still water in ponds brings a sense of depth and serenity to a garden, as well as providing an environment in which water-loving plants, ornamental fish, and other wildlife will flourish. Whether you plan to add an informal pond with its edges lost in dense clumps of iris, cattails, and grasses, or a formal water-lily pond with strong lines and clean edges, there are some general considerations to keep in mind for their design and construction:

- Locate your pond in an easily accessible spot near paths, preferably with an adjoining viewing area. The pond also should be located near sources of water (for topping up the level in the summer) and of electricity (for running pumps and outdoor lighting).

- Local codes often require that fences be built around ponds deeper than three feet — contact your local Building Department for further information. Even if permits are not required, you might consider using a pond construction as a sandbox while children are young, and then converting it to a water feature as they grow older. The natural stone fountains described on p. 134 are safe water features for a garden in which young children play.

- Plan to make your pond as large as the site reasonably can support; an expansive sheet of water looks infinitely more alluring than a constricted puddle.

- Site the pond in a low spot in the garden to replicate the way water collects and settles in the natural landscape.

- Construct the pond on freely draining soil. Unstable, shifting soil can crack the pond liner, or cause the pond's sides to cave in. See the section on Drainage in Chapter 5, p. 70 if your site is soggy. Also plan to install an overflow drain on the edge of your pond if the site will be subject to flooding once the pond is built.

- Ensure that the pond is constructed on a site where it is protected from the oily runoff from roads, and from herbicides and fertilizers that may leach from lawns.

- Site your pond in a spot that receives from five to eight hours of sun a day if you plan to stock it with fish, water lilies, and other sun-loving plants. A pond stocked with fish and aquatic plants should cover 50 square feet of surface area or more, since one smaller than that experiences too much temperature fluctuation for the health of the fish and plants.

- Construct a pond containing aquatic plants and fish to a depth between 18 and 30 inches. In order to accommodate the different growing needs of various plants, you can excavate the pond in several levels. (See steps 3 and 4 in "Constructing an Informal Pond," p. 118.) If you plan to overwinter fish in your pond in exceptionally cold regions, then excavate the pond to 2½ feet at its deepest level, where the fish can congregate safely. Reflecting ponds with no plants can be as shallow as 12 inches in depth.

- Locate your pond well away from overhanging deciduous trees and shrubs unless you are prepared to clear the water of falling leaves and other debris regularly; decaying organic material can cloud water, harm fish, and damage filters and pumps.

Informal Ponds

Informal ponds suit any garden where a natural look is desired, especially Japanese gardens, informal rock gardens, and wildlife-attracting gardens. Natural-looking ponds are usually shaped in strong, flowing lines: avoid fussy, wavering edges or any shape approaching the formal square, circle, or rectangle. Uncut stones and rocks can serve in such ponds as natural edging, stepping stones, and islands. Cobbles and gravel can serve as pond flooring and as versatile edging materials.

There are three ways to line an informal pond: concrete, prefabricated fiberglass forms, and flexible reinforced PVC or butyl rubber sheets, which will contour to the excavated hole. If you plan to use stones and rocks around or in your pond, then you may want to use the fiberglass molds or the flexible liners instead of concrete, since embedded rocks tend to pull away from the concrete during cold weather, creating cracks and leaks which are very troublesome to waterproof. Because preformed fiberglass ponds come in limited sizes and shapes, flexible liners are probably the best alternative to use in constructing naturalistic ponds. The following instructions explain how to construct an informal pond with a PVC or butyl rubber lining. (See p. 122 for instructions on how to install a preformed fiberglass pond.)

Pond liners of butyl rubber or of reinforced PVC at least 20 mils thick should last for 15 to 20 years if installed correctly. To estimate the amount of material you need to line your pond, add the pond's length to double its maximum depth, and then allow an additional two feet to create a one-foot-wide "lip" around the pond's edges. Then use the same formula to calculate the width.

For example, to estimate the lining required for a rectangular pond five feet wide by ten feet long by two feet deep (5' x 10' x 2'):

Length + (2 x depth) + 2   10 + (2 x 2) + 2 = 16
Width + (2 x depth) + 2   5 + (2 x 2) + 2 = 11

You will need a liner with dimensions of 16 x 11.

You can either buy an off-the-shelf precut liner with dimensions similar to your pond's, or get your supplier to cut a custom liner to your specifications.

Since ultraviolet rays quickly destroy flexible pond liners, it is necessary to protect the liners where they emerge from the water at the edge of the pond. See "Using Rocks and Gravel to Edge an Informal Pond," next page.

CONSTRUCTING AN INFORMAL POND

1. Install any needed drainage.
2. Outline the boundaries of the pond with rope or a garden hose.
3. Excavate the pond in several levels, with each level's walls angled at about 20 degrees (this slight angle enables ice in a frozen pond to slide up the sides as it expands, instead of piercing the liner). Since you will be installing a foundation made of old carpeting, dig each level of the pond an inch or two deeper than the final depth you want it to be (Figure 8–1).
4. Begin by creating a ledge eight to ten inches below the final water level that rims the edge of the pond: waterside and marginal plants can be established on this shelf. A second shelf, 12 to 18 inches below the final water level, will accommodate aquatics such as many varieties of water lilies. Leave the deepest level for the center of the excavation; submersible pumps should be sited here.
5. If you construct a pond whose rim is lopsided or uneven, it will remain an eyesore in the garden that will give you no peace until the problem is corrected. Since it is critical that the final water level of a pond be absolutely even, use a carpenter's level on a board to ensure accuracy at every stage of the digging.
6. Once the hole is excavated, remove any roots or stones that could pierce the pond liner, and then tamp the soil firmly.
7. Line the excavation with a layer of old carpeting laid face

Figure 8–1. Creating ledges in pond construction. Gravel and pots hold aquatic plants on ledges.

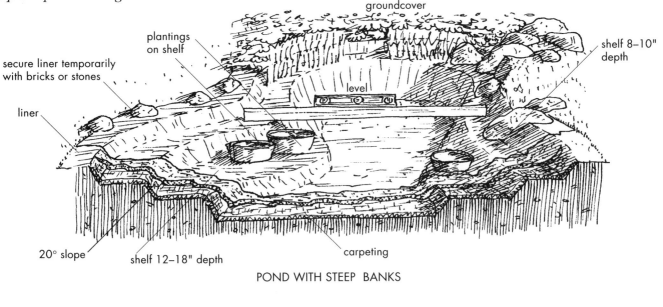

POND WITH STEEP BANKS

down. Use damp sand to fill in any dips or hollows left by the carpet layer.

8. Spread the pond lining in the excavated hole, making sure that an even "lip" about a foot wide extends over the hole's edges.

9. After securing the liner lip with bricks or stones, fill the pond with water, allowing the liner to press into its final resting place through the pressure of the water.

10. Construct the pond's edgings (see below).

Using Rocks and Gravel to Edge an Informal Pond

Pond edges are where construction details such as liners meet and blend into the garden flooring, which in a natural pond usually is composed of some combination of earth, stone, gravel, and plants. Whatever kinds of edging material you use, the liner must run up under it securely enough to remain invisible and watertight.

If the pond you are constructing has steep banks, then a combination of stones and rammed earth, anchored with groundcovers and trailing plants, makes an attractive edge. As with grouping stones on land (see Chapter 2, p. 21), use a mix of sizes and shapes of the same kind of stone, making sure their strata point in the same direction. Large, rounded stones, recliners, and low, flat-headed stones create a serene atmosphere appropriate to the rim of a placid pond; they also emphasize the horizontal lines which should dominate a pond scene.

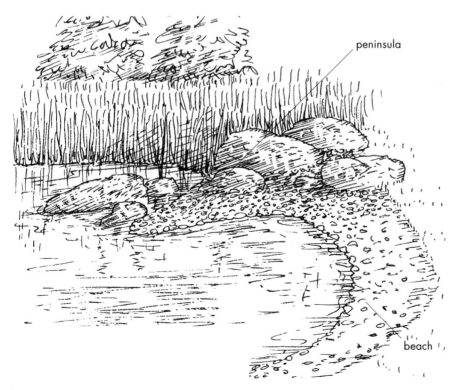

Figure 8–2. A beach and peninsula made of gravel and rock.

Half-bury the larger stones in the bank, and allow one or two to trail into the pond for a gentle transition between water and earth. Because rocks and stones may pierce flexible pond liners if there is no cushioning layer between them, put down several inches of rounded gravel layers wherever you site rocks and stones in the pond or on its immediate edges. You can establish your waterside plants on a steep bank with less fear of their eroding away by setting them in the earth in open-bottomed fiber pots: as the fiber pots slowly decompose, the plant's roots will settle into the bank.

If you want the pond to have a wide, slightly inclined, edge rather like a beach, then gravel, drain rock, and cobblestones can serve as attractive cover materials. Waterside plants can be planted directly in the selected stone material for a natural look. In addition, gravel can be used to hold waterside and bog plants in place on the shelves or ledges that rim the pond. Stones and rocks can also be used in combination with gravel or drain rock to create inlets or peninsulas around the pond's edge (see Figure 8–2 on p. 119).

Bog Gardens

Bogs occur in the natural landscape wherever fresh water saturates an area of peaty soil year-round. Unlike swamps, bogs rarely support trees; instead they act as havens for the wide variety of shrubs, grasses, and flowering plants that like to keep their feet permanently wet. In gardens, bogs make especially attractive additions to rock garden settings, where they are usually attached to ponds.

If you wish to create a bog garden adjacent to your pond, use some large stones as an informal dam between the pond and bog area. These stones should be set high enough to prevent the soil from the bog mixing into the clearer water of the pond. Excavate the bog area 14 to 18 inches deep, and line it with a flexible liner which has a few small perforations in the bottom for slow drainage. Fill in the bog with a rich, peaty soil and plant marsh marigold *(Caltha palustris)*, skunk cabbage *(Lysichiton americanum)*, moisture-loving reeds and ferns, and species of iris, monkey flower *(Mimulus)*, and primrose *(Primula)*. Top the bog off from time to time in hot, dry weather with a garden hose, making sure the soil stays constantly sodden.

Islands and Stepping Stones

Even small ponds can feature islands made from stones, either by themselves or in combination with earth and plants. Stones in tall vertical, low vertical, reclining, and flat-headed shapes make particularly attractive groupings, with the water surface acting in place of the ground line when the stones are positioned together. As with land groupings that are half buried in the ground, the island stones gain a look of massive permanence when they appear at least half submerged in the water. You can make an island slope gently into the surrounding water by using cobbles, drain rock, or gravel for a beach.

Islands made of a combination of earth and stone should be planted with grasses, pines, and other subdued plants, since bright flowers or elaborate compositions may detract from the atmosphere of serenity and simplicity that is an informal pond's chief charm.

Flat-headed stones rising at least several inches above the surface of the pond can be used as informal stepping stones. Arrange them in a naturally meandering curve rather than in a straight line, site them close enough together for a safe, comfortable passage across the water, and set them firmly on the bottom of the pond to eliminate dangerous shifting or wobbling. Again, use several inches of rounded gravel layers underneath them to prevent damage to the pond liner.

Formal Ponds

Formal ponds serve a different function in gardens from informal ponds, and different stone materials are used in their construction and ornamentation. Informal ponds soften and diffuse the garden's overall atmosphere with their asymmetrical shapes, natural borders, and teeming flora and fauna. Uncut stones and rocks, gravels with their rounded edges, and water-smoothed cobbles all look natural in such a setting.

Formal ponds, however, act as yet another hardscape in the garden, adding their clean lines and hard edges to the geometric shapes already at work in the design. Although formal ponds often feature water lilies or other aquatic plants, their chief use is as a reflecting surface, so the amount of vegetation in or near them is kept relatively sparse. Cut stone, in the form of flagstones, crazy paving, and Belgian blocks, frequently is used for edging formal ponds.

Formal ponds are often sited close to the house or other garden hardscapes, such as terraces and walls, since their straight lines and precise angles blend in gracefully with the dimensions of the other structures. If the paving surrounding the pond is kept flush with the ground, then an attractive horizontal sweep is introduced to the setting.

Squares, circles, rectangles, and octagons — these are the classic shapes of formal ponds, whether they are set flush with the earth or elevated in raised enclosures. In addition to these traditional shapes, formal ponds can be constructed in L-shapes, as squares or rectangles superimposed on one another in different levels, or even as ponds within a complex of ponds. You can construct the pond with reinforced PVC or butyl rubber, following the directions above, or use preformed fiberglass ponds that come in appropriate shapes. In order to install a fiberglass mold, use the steps that follow.

1. Excavate a hole with the same contours as the pond but several inches deeper in all dimensions. If you want the edging materials (see step 6, below) to lie flush with the ground surrounding the pond, then allow for the depth of the materials when you excavate.

2. Remove rocks and tree roots from the hole and tamp the earth firmly.

3. Spread several inches of sand over the bottom of the hole, wet it with a fine spray from the garden hose, and let it settle for 24 hours.

4. Lower the mold into the hole, then add two or three inches of water to the bottom of the mold to balance it. Level the mold, using a carpenter's level on a board.

5. Shovel sand around the sides of the mold to support them. Wet the sand down after spading it around the sides, and add more sand after 24 hours, once settling has occurred.

6. Construct the pond's edges, which can be made of mortared straight-edged flagstones, crazy paving, or Belgian blocks (see Chapter 7, pp. 110-113). Or use large stone slabs set directly into the ground for a slightly less formal look. Whichever edging material you select, be sure it overhangs the pond by several inches to conceal construction details and the mold edge.

RAISED POOLS

Raised pools suit very formal areas directly adjacent to the house, or flagstone or Belgian block terraces where limpid water

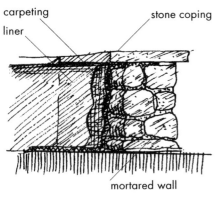

Figure 8–3. Raised pools work well in formal areas near the house.

carpeting
liner
stone coping
mortared wall

is needed to soften and enliven the surrounding stonescape (Figure 8–3); they also can serve as attractive extensions to stone walls when built of the same materials as the walls. Raised pools can be constructed in the same variety of shapes as ground-level formal ponds.

To construct the shell of a raised pool, build a mortared stone wall of rubble or ashlar that is 18 to 30 inches tall and at least 12 inches wide (see Chapter 7, pp. 99-100). Line the bottom and inner sides of the masonry shell with old carpeting and then fit reinforced PVC or butyl rubber sheets to the inside contours, tucking the excess over the top of the wall construction. Cap the stone wall with a wide coping on which it is comfortable to sit or to rest pots of plants.

A Sunken Pond

As with sunken gardens (see Chapter 9, p. 146), sunken ponds suggest an enchanted, hidden-away corner of the garden, where an especially romantic atmosphere prevails. In Figure 8–4, an octagonal pond, rimmed by three descending rows of shallow stone steps, features water lilies and a small fountain. The pond, which was designed by landscape architect Thomas Church, is sited at a low spot in the terrain, where the surrounding and enveloping shrubs and trees give it a "lost garden" setting.

Figure 8–4. A sunken octagonal pool designed by landscape architect Thomas Church.

To construct a sunken pond, begin by excavating the dimensions of two or three wide, shallow steps around the rim of the pond site, and then proceed with constructing the steps and the pond according to previous instructions. (See the Steps section in Chapter 6, pp. 91-92; also refer to the methods for constructing ponds with flexible liners, p. 118, and using fiberglass molds, p. 122).

CONVERTING A SWIMMING POOL

Increasing numbers of gardeners are turning their swimming pools into ornamental ponds, rife with water plants and darting koi. The first steps in this conversion are to dismantle diving boards and entry/exit handles, and then to paint the inside of the swimming pool, usually a bright blue, with a dark, nontoxic, waterproof paint.

Pave the area surrounding the pool with straight-edged flagstones for a formal look, or with crazy paving or irregular stone slabs for a semiformal look. Whatever material is used, make it overhang the pool by several inches for the most attractive finish. Pots filled with grasses, bamboos, and other plants with attractive foliage can be placed on the pond's edge, where they will be reflected by the surface of the water.

Figure 8–5. A swimming pool can be converted into a naturalistic pond.

In order to create a natural-looking pond out of your swimming pool, edge it with such features as boulders set in cobbles or a waterfall plunging from a stony outcrop, and use crazy paving or irregular stone slabs, thickly edged in plants, to create an asymmetrical water edge.

STREAMS

Natural streams, and those that are artfully constructed to look natural, bring a cheerful energy to the garden. Whether they run smoothly and quietly, with tiny ripples dimpling their dark surfaces, or babble comfortably as they tumble over stones and gravel, streams refresh and enliven the air and the plants around them, and also act to unify the various garden areas they wander across. Stone and gravel can play several roles in the design and construction of streams, roles that differ from the ones they play in the creation of ponds.

This is because there are different dynamics at work in each kind of water feature. A pond is a placid, unmoving body of water with a horizontal sweep. Its surface is its most important design feature, with water, plants, rocks, and their reflections creating a composition that is essentially two-dimensional — one which the viewer's eye tends to move across and over. Rocks and gravels function as edgers and liners in ponds, but their chief use as ornaments is confined to the pond's surface.

In contrast, a stream is a body of water in motion, and the viewer's eye looks down into it rather than stopping at its surface. Therefore the parts of the stone underneath the water, as well as the parts that break the surface, are visually important in the stream's design. And stones and rocks play a different function in streams because they channel the moving water, making it run faster or slower, and breaking it up into eddies and small pools. The importance of stones and gravels in the design of streams is enhanced because plants rarely play a role in moving water, remaining instead in slower, marshier areas near the stream's edge. The play of water running over or around rock, the patterns of light and shadow tumbling over the wet surfaces of stone and gravel, and the murmur of water as it meets stone are the main factors you have to work with in designing and constructing an attractive stream.

Before looking at specific techniques for constructing streams, let's look at some considerations to keep in mind when designing them:

- Follow the natural drainage patterns in your garden when laying out the run of the stream. Doing this helps to ensure that the stream will blend naturally into the landscape, and that the terrain it crosses has an adequate slope (which ideally should be in the range of 1/100).

- Keep the size of the stream in scale with the rest of the garden.
- When you design the appearance of your stream, consider the nature of the terrain along its borders. The stream that will meander through a relatively flat orchard and meadow, for example, probably should run broad, deep, and slow between even, rather level banks, while a stream that will wander down the side of a rock garden might run narrow, fast, and shallow between uneven, asymmetrical banks.
- Use sharp-edged boulders and crushed rock in streams that are meant to evoke high-country streams. In contrast, use eroded boulders, rounded gravels, and smooth cobblestones for the kinds of streams that are natural to lower-lying terrain.
- Natural streams twist and turn in the landscape but, as with paths, when you lay out a stream, be sure to make its turns few, strong, and dynamic, rather than numerous, fussy, and inconsequential.
- Vary the depth, velocity, levels, and edging characteristics of your stream as it passes through different areas in the garden.

Constructing a Natural Stream

A natural-looking constructed stream can be of any depth and width and carry low or high volumes of water, depending upon the capacity of the recirculating pump system used to move the water. But if you want to minimize both the work of excavation and the water volume in your stream, a depth ranging between four and six inches is sufficient for most of its course, with a few deeper pools dug out here and there for variety's sake.

In regions with mild winters the stream can be made watertight with a foundation of three inches of sand covered by 32 mil reinforced PVC. The liner is weighted down and protected by an inch of gravel or by cobblestones. In cold-winter regions, lay a foundation of four inches of crushed rock, topped by two inches of builder's sand, before lining the streambed with the reinforced PVC.

1. Run ropes or garden hoses along each side of your proposed streambed, widening it gently and asymmetrically at the bends. Decide on the bends where you will construct rocky outcrops, cobbled inlets, or graveled peninsulas, and leave sufficient space for these features to be added later.
2. Excavate the streambed to the final desired depth, *plus* the depth required for the foundation (see above).
3. Lay the stream liner down, and cover it with a mix of different-sized crushed rocks for a high-country stream, or by gravel, drain rock, and small cobbles for a stream meant to evoke lower terrain. When adding these materials, lay them in fairly distinct, flexible strips, as though they had

been deposited naturally in the streambed by the force of moving water.

4. To conceal the liner edges where they meet the banks of the stream, shovel a trench and fold the liner into it. Weigh down the trenched liner with stones, soil, crushed rock, or gravel, and establish plants nearby.

5. Finally, set stones in the stream or on its edges in order to channel the water in attractive patterns. The key to designing an informal stream using stone and gravel in this fashion is to see how nature uses the same materials in the natural landscape, and then to adapt those ideas to your own garden's terrain.

At different bends in the stream, for example, set stones up as small promontories, which will cause deep swirls and ripples in the water going by them. A spot on the opposite bank, just downstream, may feature a shallow inlet of sand and gravel, edged by waterside plants. Or set a large rock, surrounded by several smaller ones, near the center of the stream to create a small rapids; then, further downstream, pile some large stones opposite each other on both banks and extend them out into the stream to create a partial dam. Using stone in this way allows you to speed up or slow down the velocity of the water at various points along the course of the stream, as well as to alter how loud or soft it sounds at different spots.

Watercourses

Watercourses suit formal gardens in which moving water is wanted, but where the natural stream's meandering course would seem untidy or out of place. Edged by neatly planted flower and shrub beds, watercourses may be used as the main water feature in a garden; or they may be used as the connecting links between formal ponds and fountains in different garden "rooms." Cut stone in the form of flagstones can be used to edge a watercourse in formal style. For a formal gravel garden (see Chapter 9, p. 147), consider using Belgian blocks or quarried stones to edge

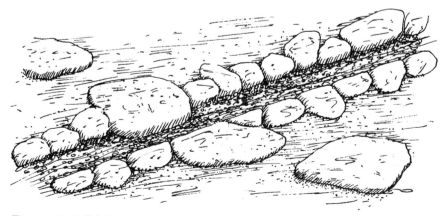

Figure 8–6. Edging a watercourse.

the watercourse; roughly shaped stones also serve as attractive edgings for channels in Japanese-style gardens (Figure 8–6).

Watercourses don't need to be especially wide or deep to make an impact. The following directions explain how to construct a channel deep enough to accommodate small aquatic plants, assuming that a recirculating pump is used to keep the water flowing and clean:

1. Outline the run of your proposed water channel with ropes or garden hoses. Excavate a level trench 12 inches deep *plus* the height of the paving materials that will edge it (see step 4 below). Slope the sides of the watercourse at a 20-degree angle.
2. After tamping the soil well, lay a foundation of three inches of builder's sand and water it to settle.
3. Line the trench with 32 mil reinforced PVC or butyl rubber, bringing the liner edges over the top of each side with about a foot to spare.
4. Construct the watercourse's edges of mortared straight-edged flagstones, quarried stones, or Belgian blocks (see Chapter 7, pp. 110-113). Whichever edging material you select, make sure it overhangs the watercourse's edges by several inches to conceal construction details and the liner.
5. Stepping stones added to a watercourse provide attractive ways to cross the water; they also set up interesting swirls and murmurs as the water flows around them.

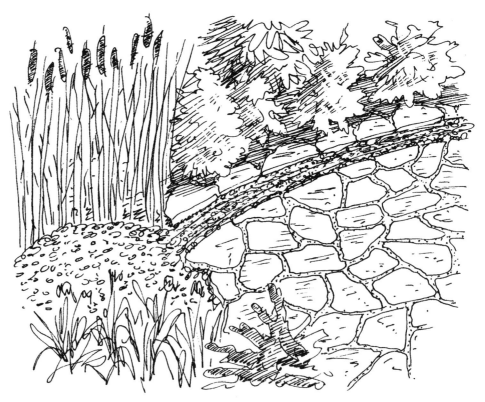

Figure 8–7. A semiformal watercourse in a landscape.

For a semiformal look, make the watercourse meander through the landscape, give it asymmetrical edges, and border it with mortared crazy paving (Figure 8–7). Terraces edged with such watercourses look especially attractive and inviting.

If you construct a watercourse along the natural drainage patterns in your garden, then it can serve to carry off excess rainwater after storms. In an area of the garden that collects excess water on a regular basis, build a sufficiently deep watercourse whose sides are made of quarried stone, and have it terminate in an attractive dry well constructed to look like a pond filled in with drain rock. Plants that thrive with wet feet, such as iris, osier dogwoods, cattails, and sedges, can be established on the edges of the dry well.

WATERFALLS

> . . . transparent, cool, and watery wealth
> Here flowing falls . . . . [1]

In these lines the poet Henry Vaughan evokes a waterfall's particular charm — that of water tumbling through time and space in splashing, sparkling abundance. Stone and water probably have their most dramatic encounters in waterfalls, whether in naturalistic settings, where white water leaps down miniature rock-strewn gorges, or in formal settings, where clear water glides smoothly over evenly stepped waterstairs made of flagstones or quarried stone slabs.

Naturalistic Waterfalls

In order to make your waterfall look as natural as possible, study how one looks and functions in the natural landscape, and then adapt those features, where possible, to your own garden. Natural waterfalls usually are formed by grade changes in streams, with boulders and stones often providing the "skeleton" over which the water falls. The height and slope of the stony skeleton (along with the volume of the water) determines the velocity and musical quality of the waterfall:

Before moving on to specific techniques for building informal waterfalls, here are several considerations to keep in mind when designing them.

- A secluded spot in the garden that features natural elevation changes is ideal. If your garden is more or less level, then pile dirt up from excavations made for ponds and streams against a garden wall to act as the base for the waterfall.

[1] Henry Vaughan, "The Water-fall," in *The Anchor Anthology of Seventeenth-Century Verse* (New York: Anchor Books, 1963), vol. 1, p. 417.

- Plan to make the waterfall in your garden part of a complex of water features. For instance, a sequence often found in the natural landscape features a stream which slightly widens and deepens into a pool just before plunging down the waterfall. At the base of the waterfall, the water may continue downstream to another waterfall. In the garden, a waterfall can be made to terminate in a pond.
- In deciding how steep to make your waterfall, consider whether you want an impressive cascade of white water or a relatively subdued and soothing trickle of water. A dramatic cascade will require high water volume and a clear drop of at least three feet. A less dramatic waterfall will require less water and only a gradual grade change.
- Select stones and rocks, preferably native to your area, that are appropriate to the setting you wish to create. If you want your waterfall to evoke a high-country torrent, then use tall vertical rocks and arching rocks with furrowed textures to replicate a stony mountain gorge. If gentler, lowland terrain is to be your setting, then rounded, water-smoothed boulders and stones will work best.
- Where you place boulders and stones in a waterfall determines both how the water flows and also what it sounds like. Since the variations in siting stones are endless, your best course may be to assemble a pile of the same kind of stones in assorted sizes and shapes and then experiment with different settings, keeping the following pointers in mind:

1. Siting the largest boulders or stones asymmetrically on each side of the major cascade both provides an attractive setting for the waterfall's focal point and prevents erosion of the nearby banks.
2. The shape and contours of the *lip stone*, the stone over which the water flows, determine how the water falls. If the lip stone is flat, smooth, and hangs over the rest of the waterfall, then water will fall over it in a vertical curtain. If the lip stone is rough, rounded, and set well back, then the water will slip over and down its face in broken patterns.
3. Stones set into the face of the cascade itself can separate the fall of water into attractive patterns.
4. Siting flat or reclining stones at the base of the falls makes the water recoil and foam at the point of impact.

Constructing a Naturalistic Waterfall

1. Excavate the course of the waterfall to the desired depth and contours, and ram the earth firmly. This is the point at which to bury the water conduit, usually made of PVC piping, which leads from the pump in the pond up to the small pond or stream that feeds the waterfall. Bury the piping where it will be possible to gain access to it without

major reexcavation, in case of malfunctions later on. Lay several inches of sand over the excavated area, wetting it to settle.

2. Line the course of the waterfall with 32 mil reinforced PVC, tucking the edges of the liner out of sight under the stones, earth, and plants that will border the waterfall. If the waterfall will terminate in a pond, then do the excavation and foundation laying for both features at the same time, so a single liner can be used to make them watertight. If more than one piece of liner must be used, then overlap the sheets with wide margins, making sure each sheet tucks over the top of the sheet below it for maximum waterproofing.

Most water garden experts recommend that the pond be made three to four times as large as the waterfall, so there will always be sufficient water to recirculate from pond to waterfall through the pump.

3. Arrange the rocks and stones around the waterfall as desired, making sure the liner is cushioned by several inches of rounded gravel wherever sharp rocks will be sited on it.

4. As with dry walls or natural outcrops, arrange the waterfall rocks so they remain stable by the way they fit together and by the force of gravity. It may be necessary to cement some rocks together, however, and, in such cases, seal the cement with a waterproof sealer annually.

5. Once you have the boulders and major stones sited, pause long enough in the construction process to send water down the falls, either through the pump or, if it has not been installed yet, a garden hose. Then site the rest of the stones in order to achieve attractive flow patterns and "white" noise.

6. Construct edgings around the pond of stones, gravel, and plants (see p. 119).

Formal Waterfalls

Formal waterfalls, resembling a series of shallow, evenly spaced terraces or stairs, suit formal sites, where their symmetrical lines and clean edges complement other formal water features and blend into the overall garden design. A flight of waterstairs can be built where a watercourse undergoes a grade change, for instance, or to join two formal ponds that are constructed on different levels (see Figure 8–8, next page). However you choose to add waterstairs to another feature, make sure that the materials used in both features complement each other. For a watercourse bordered by formal flagstones, for example, add a waterstairs made from the same kind of stone, perhaps hewn into thicker slabs for a pleasing contrast.

Figure 8-8. Mortared stonework channels a formal watercourse.

To construct waterstairs, follow instructions for building flagstone steps in Chapter 6, p. 92. Between steps 2 and 3, lay a liner of 32 mil reinforced PVC down to ensure watertightness. Paint the mortar or cement used in constructing your waterstairs with a water sealer annually. For a semiformal waterstairs, follow the instructions for constructing a flight of stepping stones — Chapter 6, p. 89 — with the addition of a lining of reinforced PVC spread over the foundation of crushed rock and builder's sand.

A less elaborate formal waterfall can be fashioned from a roughly quarried stone slab, which is gently inclined between two levels of a watercourse so that water can glide down its furrows in pleasing patterns. Such a feature is evocative of the water chutes common to Middle Eastern paradise gardens, which were stone slabs carved with patterns to make water fall in decorative scallops and flounces.

Water Features for Xeriscapes

Cascades of crushed rock, torrents of cobbles, and swirled pools of gravel — stone materials can be used to lend the dynamic, invigorating qualities of water even to the dry features found in xeriscapes. Such stonescapes can be added to gardens where it is impossible to bring in water to the site, or where the gardener chooses to conserve water exclusively for irrigating plants.

In constructing a "dry" pond, stream, or waterfall, you can adapt the techniques given above for building water features, with the difference that watertight liners and sealed cements or mortars are unnecessary. Where you would have placed a liner, you can lay down a plastic sheet to help suppress weeds. But in *designing* such features, it may be helpful to keep the following considerations in mind.

In one kind of dry stonescape, say a streambed, the stones and rocks will be sited in such a way as to replicate the skeleton or foundation of a stream, rather than the water on the stream's surface. Stone materials are sited in such a feature as they would be in "wet" streams, where the force of the water tends to distri-

Figure 8-9. A dry streambed composed of rocks and cobbles.

Natural Stone Fountains

Carved stone fountains and statuary have dominated the water features on display in formal western gardens from the period of the Renaissance on. But today, many gardeners prefer the informal look of natural stone when they come to install fountains in their own yards. Here are three fountains that will suit natural gardens, Japanese gardens, and most other gardens with an informal style.

1. Cobblestone fountain. This simple and attractive fountain features a jet of recirculating water which shoots up into the air to fall back onto cobblestones. The water jet can range in height and force from a bubble to a geyser. Plants in containers that are buried in the cobblestones soften the scene.

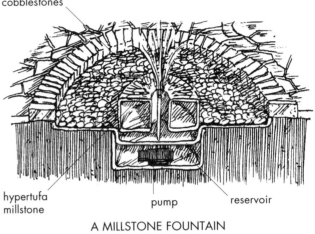

A MILLSTONE FOUNTAIN

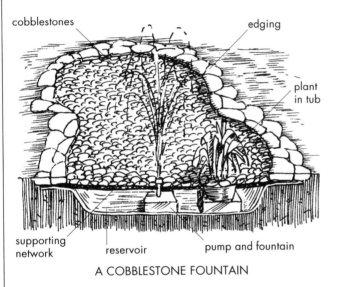

A COBBLESTONE FOUNTAIN

2. Millstone fountain. This design is based on the same principles as the cobblestone fountain, but it features a water jet that spurts from a millstone. To make a millstone from hypertufa material, follow the directions for making stepping stones given in Chapter 10, p. 154, with the amendments that a millstone should be at least three inches thick, and that a hole for the water jet should be created in the center of the millstone by using a round, plastic-wrapped object, such as a pint ice cream container, set in the mold when the hypertufa mix is poured.

3. Stone water fountain. A stone set in gravel or cobbles over a reservoir and pump may have its center carved out so that water seeps slowly down its sides as from a natural spring . Or the stone's center may feature a narrow, hollow core, from which the water jet bubbles directly onto the stone's surface to run down its sides.

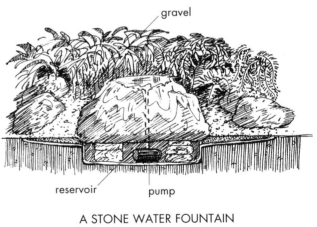

A STONE WATER FOUNTAIN

bute them in flexible strips. In effect, the stream is designed so viewers are conscious that they are looking down into the bed or underside of the stream, and their minds' eyes will bring water into the stream to complete the scene. This kind of dry stonescape engages the viewers' imaginations by making them supply something which ought to be in the landscape, but is not.

In contrast, a second kind of dry stonescape uses sand, chippings, gravel, drain rocks, or cobbles to replace water in a scene. In such a feature, the stone materials are used in a different way than in the first type. In a stream where cobbles are used to replace water, for example, the cobbles may be shiny and pointed in one direction, as if to symbolize rippling water. They will also fill the streambed as full as water does in a wet stream. In this second type of feature, stone materials are used to emulate the surface of the water, rather than the bottom of the streambed (see Figure 8–9 on p. 133).

Similarly, where stone features are meant to evoke the skeleton of a waterfall, boulders can be stepped in such a way that it is easy to imagine sparkling water plunging over and around them. Lilyturfs, sedums, or ornamental grasses can be used in such features to evoke flowing water. In a waterfall where water is actually to be represented by stone materials, however, small cobbles will cascade down the rock surfaces, plunging into a pool where gravel is raked to replicate the ripples one finds on the surface of the pond water.

CHAPTER 9

ROCK GARDENS

In *My Rock Garden*, published in 1907, the plant explorer Reginald Farrer describes his first glimpse of an alpine flower for which he had been scouring the slopes of the Meiden Pass, some 9,000 feet above the Rhone Valley in central Germany: "Ah, *Eritrichium nanum* is near! Down, beating heart! In another moment I am on my knees before the nearest tuft of blue, babbling inanities into its innumerable lovely faces. Ah, the blessed little creature, how it takes one captive! So exquisite, so tiny, this indomitable small soul that sits up here on the barren slope from age to age!"

Farrer's outburst captures the intensity of the passion which swept British horticultural circles in the early twentieth century for high-country plants, a passion which led to radically new developments in the construction of the rockery.

Although Farrer and other experts noted early on that a surprising number of these plants will adapt to lowland soils and garden conditions quite happily, most alpines and rock plants maintain a reputation for being fussy about their growing environments, and for flourishing best in conditions that give them sharp drainage for their roots and perfectly dry crowns and leaves for most of the year. They often need, in short, a setting that replicates their original growing environments on the stony outcrops and screes of mountains. By the turn of the twentieth century, British gardeners, in their efforts to grow alpines in lowland areas, were devising varieties of rock gardens that were more or less geologically accurate renditions of the alpine's original homes.

This enthusiasm for alpine plants displayed in rocky settings crossed the Atlantic to American shores by the 1920s and '30s. Here, in subsequent decades, it met with and was influenced by another gardening tradition that emphasizes the use of stone — Japanese gardening. In this gardening style, stone features are created to evoke "natural scenes" from a variety of altitudes and terrains in the natural landscape, from stone-choked mountain streams to quiet forest glens, where boulders lie in the tall grasses as placidly and grandly as sleeping bears and tigers. In these "scenes," plants often play a secondary role to the stone, a reversal of the relationship as it developed in most western rock gardens (see the box on p. 138).

Separately and in their numerous hybrid descendants, the British and Japanese traditions have led to a wide variety of approaches for designing rock gardens in the United States, ranging from strictly utilitarian cradles for alpines to subtle, abstract compositions balancing stone, water, alpines, and a variety of other plants, including bulbs, grasses, succulents, dwarf conifers, and groundcovers.

INFORMAL ROCK GARDENS: GARDENS OF THE MOUNTAINS

Let's start with a look at how to design and construct high-country settings, such as rocky outcrops, screes, and upland meadows. Before we consider construction techniques for each specific type, the following are some general design principles to keep in mind for them all:

- Don't stint on space when designing a high-country rock garden. Nature scatters her screes, meadows, and rocky outcrops over a massive canvas and, although few gardeners have the room to replicate natural stone features on a similar scale, there should be enough space in the designed rock garden to convey some of the atmosphere of windswept grandeur that haunts an upland scene.

- Give it a natural, open setting, one well away from trees and large shrubs, with their dense shade, dripping leaves, and invading roots. This is advice first promulgated by Reginald Farrer, and it has been followed with profit by generations of rock gardeners ever since. Farrer also suggested siting natural rock gardens away from buildings or other formal structures. Outcrops of rock and gravel wedged against a house, or between the swimming pool and the garage, for instance, usually look contrived and unattractive. And, on a practical note, most alpines grow best in an environment where there are cooling air currents constantly playing across them, a condition difficult to replicate in an enclosed space bordered by buildings.

- Integrating a rock garden with the rest of the garden can be tricky — for instance, the transition from a dry, gravelly scree to lush sweeps of lawn looks unnatural and can lead to a choppy, awkward feeling in a garden. Use transitional features, such as paths and terraces made of gravel or stone paving slabs, to smooth or blur the point at which the rock garden and other garden areas meet. Planting up such features with alpines and rock plants, or with sympathetic companion plants, such as succulents, drought-tolerant groundcovers, and ornamental herbs, also ties the areas together visually.

- When you construct the rock garden, give it numerous different angles and exposures, ranging from full sun and

Adapting the Stone Gardening Traditions of Japan to Western Rock Gardens

Holy mountains, abstract sculptures, and the bones of dragons: as we have seen in chapters 1 and 2, the Asian tradition for using rock in gardens is ancient, complex, and highly sophisticated. But what relevance does it have for western rock gardens?

First of all, rocks and stones bear highly charged symbolic meanings in Asian gardens which cannot, and probably should not, be imported wholesale into western gardens. But adopting the general proposition that stone is a magical, evocative garden material can open western gardeners' eyes to using it in decorative new ways in their own landscapes.

Finding the exotic stones and constructing the elaborate "mountains" and grottos of Chinese gardens may be beyond the ambitions or inclinations of most western gardeners, but many Japanese approaches to using stone import well into gardens wholly western in design and atmosphere. And it proves surprisingly straightforward to put those approaches into practice, using the following principles as guidelines.

1. Respect the conditions and appearance of the site and its surrounding landscape. Use stone and rock native to the area, or choose non-native stone having a color, shape, and texture that harmonizes with the site.
2. Use nature as a guide when positioning rocks in the garden. The fundamental aim is to arrange rocks and stones to look as though they have been there forever.
3. Avoid mixing different types of stone and rock in the same feature. If they must be mixed, match them closely for compatible colors, textures, and shapes.

4. When piling rocks together, make sure the striations and furrows of each rock point in the same direction. This avoids a crazy-quilt effect, and makes the feature look as though it is all part of the same naturally occurring outcrop.
5. Set stones and rocks into the landscape as if they were icebergs, with only the tips showing. The aim of setting stones into their site is to make them look solid and stable, like naturally occurring features.
6. Use stones and stone features with broad, horizontal lines to create a sense of tranquility and serenity in the rock garden. Use low, flat-headed rocks, large, rounded rocks, and reclining rocks as the major stones in the composition, with a few tall, vertical stones added for accent and variety.
7. Keep a pleasing balance between rock features and plants in the design. Too much rock in a garden composition makes it heavy and overwhelming; too little makes it seem frivolous and unconvincing. Since every site is different, there can be no hard and fast rules in this matter, but keeping the stone covering more than 20 percent and less than 40 percent of an area will probably result in the most satisfying balance.
8. Use stone to reveal the essence of other garden features. Flowing water and ephemeral flowers, for instance, provide stone with evocative contrasts in form, texture, and mood.

By adopting such principles, western gardeners can create stone features that offer not only practical solutions to site problems, but ones that add stability, tranquility, and beauty to the landscape as well.

wind to sheltered shade. Create separate "pockets" for different growing mediums, from sharply drained gravelly mixtures to moist, comparatively rich soils composed of organic materials. Providing a variety of growing conditions means you will have just the right spot for establishing any kinds of plants that happen to intrigue you in the future, without having to rebuild areas of the rock garden to accommodate them.

- Since most alpines and rock plants are quite dainty, construct paths so that visitors can get up close to the plants on display. Paths should also be sited to make it easy for you to work in the rock garden. Once you have decided where the paths will run, construct them with good drainage and firm foundations, since paths can become impromptu watercourses in sudden downpours, especially in hilly terrain. Gravel paths and stepping stones work especially well in rock gardens (see Chapter 6).

- Consider adding water features. Trickling streams, resembling runoff from glaciers, or peaty ponds, like those sometimes found in alpine meadows, will add movement, sound, and scintillating light to a stony scene (see Chapter 8 for stream and pond construction).

- As with any stone feature, using native materials will ensure a natural and harmonious effect.

- Take nature as your guide in selecting which type of stone to use in your constructed feature — worn and rounded stone looks natural when used to form an eroded outcrop or an alpine meadow, while sharply angled stone often looks just right in screes.

- Many gardeners recommend using porous stone for rock gardens, such as limestone and certain kinds of sandstone, because they provide the kind of quick-draining environment that alpines and rock plants love. But Vermont and New Hampshire gardeners report wonderful results from snuggling high-country plants around dense granites and gneiss; so it's worth experimenting on a small scale with whatever rock is commonly available in your area before investing in imported limestones or sandstones.

- Once they have gained a grip, weeds and stray grass are extremely difficult to eradicate from a rock garden. Make sure that the soils you use in construction are free of the seeds and roots of any kind of weed or undesirable plant.

A Natural Rocky Outcrop

Gardeners fortunate enough to have gardens with naturally occurring outcrops need only exploit what nature already has bestowed upon them. Often these natural outcrops occur in clumps and drifts, with the connecting bedrock buried under lawns by previous homeowners. By tearing out the lawn and exposing the connecting links, and by digging out any lowland plants previously planted in the ridges and crevices of the main outcrop, you can create a healthy environment for alpines and rock plants.

To enlarge such natural outcrops, remove the garden soil around their peripheries to a depth of at least 18 inches (excavate to 24 inches in wet climates or soggy soils), and lay a foundation of six inches of crushed rock, topped by two inches of fine gravel or coarse builder's sand. On top of the drainage layer, half-bury smaller rocks of the same kind as are in your outcrop, positioning them so they look naturally deposited there by the forces of erosion and gravity. Fill in the areas between the rocks with appropriate soil mixtures (see the box on p. 143), tamping soil down firmly around the rocks to eliminate air pockets.

Rock gardeners sometimes also enlarge the growing areas available to them by splitting their larger boulders with a hammer and wedge, filling the resulting crevices with a gravelly soil and planting alpines or rock plants with shallow roots in them.

CONSTRUCTING A ROCKY OUTCROP ON A SLOPE

If your garden has no natural stone outcrop but does contain banks, hillocks, or areas with any other type of significant grade change, then these are the best spots in which to design and construct your rocky outcrop.

Since your major design concern here is to make the feature look as natural as possible, study rock outcrops as they appear in the natural landscape. Such outcrops almost invariably look like the exposed tips of a huge mass of buried rock, tips that are worn down and eroded by time and the elements.

To replicate such an effect, grade your site to a gentle slope no greater than 45 degrees. Take care to leave space for a relatively flat area several feet wide at the bottom of the slope, which will tie the outcrop to the rest of the garden when mulched with a fine gravel and then planted up as the last step in construction.

Excavate the contours of the slope at least 18 inches deep. Then lay a drainage layer of six inches of crushed rock topped by two inches of fine gravel or coarse sand, burying a few large rocks beneath this layer as stable foundations under the spots where you plan to position the major exposed stones or boulders in the composition.

Most natural outcrops feature one or two large boulders, set among smaller stones which have fallen away from the main mass due to gravity and erosion. When constructing your outcrop, position the major boulders, canting them slightly upwards and inwards so rain will naturally run along their surfaces to the plant roots nearby: then carefully set a few smaller stones around them, preferably at their bases. Fill in the crevices between the stones with an appropriate soil mix (see the box on p. 143), tamping it firmly so no air pockets remain. If you use a stratified stone, such

Figure 9–1. Positioning a stony outcrop on a sloping site.

as limestone or sandstone, position all the rocks so that their strata lie on the same angle, as though an earthquake had heaved them into place simultaneously (Figure 9–1).

Constructing a Rock Garden on a Level Site

If you have a flat site on which you wish to build a rock garden, use a construction technique first developed by ancient Chinese gardeners to introduce different levels to the composition by digging out low areas and then mounding the excavated earth into ridges and plateaus above them. Use half-buried, weathered stones to replicate outcrops, and work from the bottom of the rock garden toward the top.

The most successfully designed rock gardens look massive, tranquil, and inevitable, yet it is fatally easy to construct a busy, hectic stonescape by using too many small stones and positioning them so that there is no apparent natural association either among the individual stones or between the stones and the rest of the site. A few large boulders with a litter of smaller stones and gravel at their base will look more natural and more restful than a hodgepodge of smaller stones flung about in small heaps or, even worse, rocks evenly spaced in rows, like gravestones. Or you can use flat sedimentary stones to establish a restful horizontal or tiered effect, varying the height from outcrop to outcrop for a natural look.

Some gardeners who are starting with a flat site eliminate large-scale excavation and rock moving by using old tires as the foundation for their rock gardens. They form the base of their mound on level soil with the tires, which are then filled with gravel, sand, or crushed rock. After building up several layers of tires in a rough mound, the entire construction is covered with a good, porous soil, and then rocks are buried in it according to the design principles outlined above.

Figure 9–2. A rock garden with a foundation of tires. In the upper part of the drawing, small outcrops near the main rockery tie the rockery to the rest of the garden.

Because this type of construction builds only up, and not down, from level ground, it can easily seem like an irrelevant bump in the garden, with no natural ties to the surrounding terrain. You can avoid this effect by establishing a few low outcrops on its peripheries and backfilling behind them to create minor slopes or plateaus (Figure 9–2).

Screes

True alpines, those plants which are found above the tree line on mountains, cling to rock- and gravel-strewn upland slopes called *screes*. Constructing replicas of these features permits you to grow rare alpine treasures from exotic mountain ranges half a world away, right in your own backyard.

Screes occur in the natural landscape where frost shattering has caused an accumulation of angular rock fragments at the base of a mountain slope. Plants with special needs for quick drainage and dry crowns, such as certain types of bellflowers *(Campanula garganica, C. pusilla)*, pinks *(Dianthus arenarius, D. sylvestris)*, candytuft *(Iberis saxatilis)*, and phlox *(Phlox subulata, P. douglasii)*, love to dig their vigorous, deep roots into the scree's gravelly debris.

To replicate a scree in your rock garden, site it at the base of a rocky outcrop, or in the depression between two outcrops, preferably in an area that is sunny and airy. In regions where the noon sun is strong, an eastern or northern exposure for the scree will protect delicate alpines from desiccation or sunburn, although most plants native to the upland areas of the Mediterranean or the American Southwest will benefit from a full western or southern exposure as long as they are adequately watered.

After determining the scree's boundaries, excavate the soil to 24 inches, then lay down a drainage layer of six inches of coarse crushed rock, topped with two inches of coarse builder's sand. Position a few stones for stability and variety on the drainage layer and then fill in around them with a soil mix composed of one part good garden loam to one part chopped leaves or damp peat moss to three parts fine gravel (between ⅛ inch and ½ inch in size.) Top this layer of soil with a one-inch mulch of fine gravel, which will ensure that the alpine's crown and leaves stay dry. Matching the color of the mulch gravel to the color of the stones in the rest of the rock garden will result in a harmonious composition.

Planting a Rock Garden

The key to establishing and maintaining healthy high-country plants in rock gardens is to provide them with the right kinds of soils and moisture levels. A good, all-around soil mix for most alpines will drain sharply, and is not too rich or fertile: one part good garden loam (free of weeds) to one part finely chopped leaves to one part fine gravel or coarse sand should work well for most varieties of alpines or rock plants. If you are gardening with lime lovers, which the majority of high-country plants are, then add two or three cups of ground limestone to a wheelbarrowful of the soil mix, especially if you live in an area with naturally acidic soil.

If you plan to garden with acid-loving plants, such as heathers and the dwarf rhododendrons, use a planting mix of one part good garden loam to one part coarse sand to three parts finely chopped leaves or damp peat moss. Use an appropriate fertilizer, diluted to half-strength, during the growing season. (If you expect to specialize in acid-loving plants in your garden, use a type of stone other than limestone for your rock formations, since

flaking limestone affects the pH level of the soil around it to the detriment of acid-lovers.)

In their natural settings, alpines and rock plants receive fairly consistent watering during the growing season, whether from rain or, in some sites, from glacier meltwater running about a foot below ground surface. Most regions of the United States experience enough rain during the spring to satisfy the requirements of upland plants, but a good watering system is needed in many areas to help them cope with the rigors of hot lowland summers with little consistent rain.

Some gardeners bury networks of perforated garden hoses surrounded by several inches of fine gravel near the surface of the rock garden, making sure the connecting end is exposed just above ground level at a point where a supply hose can be coupled to it at watering time. Alpines and rock plants also receive a consistent misting in the natural landscape through mountain fogs; misting them in your rock garden on the evenings of particularly hot days results in happier, healthier plants.

To make sure the scree's plants receive copious but quick-draining moisture during the growing season, install a buried watering system, as outlined in "Planting a Rock Garden," p. 143, or water by hose on a daily basis during hot dry spells. (This is a great time to examine and enjoy your little horticultural gems at a leisurely pace!)

A Rocky Meadow

Gardeners who have a more or less level site, lean soil, and a taste for grasses, wildflowers, bulbs, and groundcovers, can create a rocky meadow, a feature that will enable them to exploit their interests and growing conditions in an attractive and unusual way.

In the natural landscape, rocky meadows are found in sub-alpine terrain, where rock particles wash down from the outcrops and screes above them to mix with the decayed plant material naturally found in the meadow area itself. This soil will support a wide variety of native grasses and wildflowers, as well as those rock plants and alpines which, drifting down from the mountain slopes above, are especially vigorous and competitive.

You can recreate some of the appearance and atmosphere of an alpine meadow by embedding low, natural-looking outcrops of stratified stone, rounded fieldstones, or glacial boulders on the site and allowing rock plants, hardy alpines, and sun-loving groundcovers to nestle in their cracks and fissures, and around their bases.

To provide the right growing medium for the rest of the meadow, excavate the entire area to a depth of 18 inches, then spread a layer of several inches of gravel or small crushed rocks. On top of this layer, spread the all-around soil mix described in the box on p. 143.

There is a growing body of knowledgeable gardeners who plant up their meadow gardens with wildflowers and grasses native to their area, following a cyclical regime of burning off or scything and reseeding the site (see the bibliography for recommended books on the subject). An alternative to such an approach is to plant the meadow in drifts of ornamental grasses, naturalizing bulbs, and such flowering perennials as purple coneflower *(Echinacea purpurea)*, gayfeather *(Liatris spicata)*, black-eyed Susan *(Rudbeckia hirta)*, and goldenrod *(Solidago* spp.*).*

Depending on the size of the meadow you wish to create, gravel paths can wind between the stone features, with the taller grasses and flowering perennials screening off one part of the meadow from another. Pines and other conifers reminiscent of the high country can be used as accents within a large meadow or at its borders, while a pond, stream, or dry streambed of pebbles or cobbles will add a refreshing hint of moving water to the scene.

Combining High-Country Features in the Garden

One of the real delights of designing rock gardens is creating a combination of high-country features within a comparatively small garden area. For instance, the highest point in a rock garden can represent a rocky outcrop, with a gravelly scree fanning out from its base. A bog or pond at the bottom of the scree can catch any spillover left from watering the scree above and also act as a natural border to a rocky meadow, filled with blooms, below it. As long as each feature is in scale with the others, such a scene can take up an entire garden or a relatively small corner within it.

Many gardeners who are intrigued by alpines and rock plants feel they can't establish an informal rock garden, either because their sites are small and closely abut buildings and walls, or because they previously have established a formal style and atmosphere in the garden whose straight lines and precise angles they wish to preserve throughout. If this describes your situation, you can still create a rock garden in harmony with its surroundings by using formal constructions such as raised beds, planted dry stone walls, and terraced sunken gardens.

Raised Beds and Dry Stone Walls

One of the most attractive garden plans I have seen recently will convert a small urban lot exclusively to the growing of alpines and wall and rock plants. The 20' x 20' site originally featured a wooden deck, bordered by some overgrown shrubs in a heavy clay soil. The homeowners removed the deck and shrubs to open up the space, and are in the process of constructing dry walls and raised beds to create a healthy growing environment for their new charges.

Now the garden's southeastern boundary will be a 5½-foot-high mortared wall of roughly shaped limestone blocks, to trap the warm, strong morning and noon sun. The wall's wide coping will support several elevated hypertufa troughs spilling over with flowering alpine daphnes (*Daphne sericea*), alyssums (*Alyssum montanum*), and silvery saxifrages (*Saxifraga cotyledon pyramidalis*). Two parallel raised beds, each 30 inches high and five feet wide, are being built out from the wall at right angles, like arms outstretched before it.

The raised beds, also made of limestone, and laid dry and battered slightly toward their tops, will be planted in cascading wall plants, with sprays of *Helianthemum alpestre* 'Serpyllifolium's yellow flowers and the azure buds of *Lithodora oleifolium* making an especially striking combination. (See Chapter 7, p. 103 for construction and planting of dry stone walls.)

The owners plan to fill the beds with a 12-inch layer of rubble and crushed rock for drainage, topped with a porous soil mix (see the box on p. 143), in which some small rocks will be buried almost to their tips to provide cool root runs. These beds, which actually act as formalized screes, will eventually become encrusted by a thick, shaggy embroidery of alpines, sedums, and rock plants that scramble over their edges and down into the interstices of the wall below.

More troughs and slab gardens will nestle around the base of each bed, resting on some of the same limestone blocks that compose the walls behind them. A pea gravel with warm brown undertones that harmonizes with the limestone beds and walls will be used to mulch the beds and the garden floor around them. Velvet sedum *(Sedum dasyphyllum)* will creep through the gravel flooring and onto the troughs and raised-bed walls above them, uniting the various stone features under its dense and springy green mats.

The owners of this small, urban rock garden say that, if they had more room, their next project would be a double dry stone wall built on an east-west axis, so they could grow more sun-loving wall plants on the southern exposure and a variety of ferns, mosses, and woodland groundcovers on the shady north wall.

Sunken Gardens

To my mind, the term "sunken garden" has a mysterious air to it, conjuring up visions of deep-sea fish wiggling languidly through a drowned landscape.

In reality, sunken gardens are simply areas of the garden deliberately designed to sink below the surrounding terrain, and they are usually reached by going down a flight of steps. Whether they started out as natural depressions that were later enlarged, or were excavated in their entirety, most sunken gardens are rather formal in shape, often forming circles, squares, or rectangles whose boundaries are terraced retaining walls. The floors of most formal sunken gardens are level and can either be filled with planting beds, paved with stone slabs, or covered in gravel. Some large sunken gardens also feature pools crowded with water lilies or cattails.

Although they can also be built of brick or railroad ties, the most atmospheric retaining walls for sunken gardens are made of stone. Whether composed of formal mortared ashlar or informal rubble, stone creates the perfect frame for the plants and water features that are a sunken garden's main attractions. In cold and rainy climates, sunken gardens are sometimes sited to act as sun traps, with their stone retaining walls and flagstones soaking up the sun's warmth and radiating it to the nearby earth and plants.

If you plan to make a sunken garden deeper than three feet, then construct two or three descending tiers of low retaining walls, with wide planting beds situated between them. Establishing the same varieties of plants in natural drifts both in the beds and in the walls above and below them gives a visual flow and unity to the entire composition.

A sunken garden, with its somewhat removed or detached relationship to the main garden, may also be the perfect spot to create an informal rockery in an otherwise formal garden. In such a design natural boulders and rocks, well-embedded into gentle slopes and surrounded by alpines, bulbs, small grasses, groundcovers, and wall and rock plants, take the place of formal retaining walls. Success in designing such an informal stonescape depends, to a great extent, on making sure the slopes are gradual, rather than narrow and steep, and ensuring that the well-buried stones play a firmly secondary role to that of the plants.

Such an informal rock garden can feature either a level gravel floor, perhaps punctuated with hypertufa troughs, or informal paths, made of stepping stones or gravel, winding across a slightly bermed and thickly planted floor.

Gravel Gardens

A gravel garden combines attractive features from both rock gardens and gravel terraces.

Like a rock garden, the gravel garden can be either formal, featuring low walls and raised beds made from cut stone, or informal, featuring outcrops of natural stones and boulders. Like a gravel terrace, the gravel garden is low-maintenance, easy to install, and relatively inexpensive.

Best of all, in using gravel as its floor, the gravel garden provides good growing conditions for the wide variety of plants that like good drainage and dry stems, crowns, and leaves. Gravel also serves in this type of garden as a visually unifying and attractive backdrop, and as a water-conserving and weed-suppressing mulch.

In laying out your gravel garden:

- Decide where the paths will go first, and install good drainage and a firm foundation under them. If you construct the paths from straight-edged stone slabs or crazy paving, make sure that a high-enough edging separates the gravel from the path — strayed gravel scattered over flat stone is loud and can be slippery when walked on. If you construct the paths from gravel, then be sure their boundaries are clear, since visitors could wander off them onto graveled planting beds whose plants have not yet emerged. In such a case, place stepping stones along the run of the gravel path, or edge it with buried railroad ties, Belgian blocks, or bricks.
- Once gravel is laid down it's hard to work the soil beneath it. Therefore it is important to make sure your soil is adequately porous and free of weeds before covering it up with gravel. If your soil is soggy, consult the section on Drainage in Chapter 5, p. 70. If you have a bad weed problem, the most foolproof way to eradicate them may be to cover the area with black plastic, firmly weighted down, for an entire growing season.
- Add any desired stone features. If you plan an informal gravel garden, adding stony outcrops (see pp. 137-142) will provide attractive environments for alpines and rock plants. If you plan a formal gravel garden, low stone walls and raised beds can add interesting level changes to the otherwise flat terrain.

Estimating Gravel

1. Multiply the length of the area to be covered by its width.
2. Multiply the resulting figure by the decimal number below which corresponds to your desired depth of gravel.

Depth in Inches	Decimal Number
1	.083
2	.17
3	.25
4	.33
5	.42
6	.50
7	.58
8	.67
9	.75
10	.84
11	.92
12	1.

3. To express the product in cubic yards, the measure in which gravel usually is sold, divide it by 27.

- Gravel gardeners usually recommend laying down between two and four inches of gravel to provide an adequate mulch for most plants and common garden conditions. The "Estimating Gravel" box on p. 147 explains how to esti - mate the amount of gravel required for your garden.

The low-maintenance gravel garden discussed in Chapter 4, p. 48, lists some of the many plants that flourish especially well in gravel gardens.

Slab Gardens

For most rock gardeners, a great part of the charm of alpines and rock plants resides in their miniature size, and a great part of the charm of designing rock gardens lies in miniaturizing alpine scenes. Slab gardening represents the ultimate reduction of compact plants and rocky landscapes into small spaces.

Developed in England during the 1930s, slab gardens are made of thick, straight-edged stone slabs, whose walls are made of pieces of irregular, flattish rock cemented to the slab. Several inches of gravel are laid on top of the slab, and then a quick-draining soil mix covers the gravel. Because the rock walls are natural rather than cut, the spaces between where they join are large enough to provide free drainage. Slab gardens are often elevated on stone blocks to promote even better drainage.

Traditional slab gardens usually create a miniaturized land-scape, using tiny rock outcrops and dwarf conifers, such as *Juniperus communis* 'Compressa' and dwarf spruce *Picea abies* 'Nidiformis' to represent a mountain scene. Low mat plants, such as creeping thyme *(Thymus serpyllum)*, and stone- or gravel-loving mosses that tolerate some sun and dryness, such as *Ceratodon purpureus*, make good "shrubs" for these tableaux.

Slab gardens can be positioned on sunny stone or gravel ter-races, at the base of screes, or in front of a stone wall.

CHAPTER 10

HANDMADE STONE:
Using Hypertufa in the Garden

HYPERTUFA IS A COMBINATION of cement, peat moss, and sand that can be molded to make plant containers or other garden ornaments that look like weathered stone. Alpinists and rock plant enthusiasts have used hypertufa for many years to create plant containers, but the mix is versatile, and can also be used to fashion stepping stones and birdbaths. If you think of hypertufa as a kind of moldable stone, then only your molds, and your imagination, limit how it can be used.

Hypertufa mix was developed originally as a response to the demand among alpine and rock plant gardeners for plant containers which could provide the special growing conditions needed by their temperamental charges. Because alpines and rock plants crave sharp drainage and like to nestle their roots close to rock or stone, early efforts to cultivate them in clay or wood containers had only mixed success.

Starting in the early decades of this century, English gardeners discovered that old stone sinks from cottage kitchens and limestone and sandstone troughs, which had been used to feed and water livestock in the English countryside for centuries, made ideal containers for alpines and rock plants because they replicated the plants' natural environment and growing conditions. Soon alpinists were scouring the countryside in search of these prized stone sinks and troughs, which as a consequence became quite scarce by the 1930s. (Of course, gardeners will always prove ingenious when it comes to providing the right environment for their plants: one committed alpinist uses a sixth-century Anglo-Saxon sarcophagus that is seven feet long to cradle his!)

At this point some enterprising gardeners developed the hypertufa mixture and began producing containers that looked like the stone ones in order to meet continuing demand. The peat moss and sand in the hypertufa containers duplicate the porous growing environment of the natural limestone or sandstone of real troughs and sinks. And, like the true stone texture of troughs and sinks, the stonelike texture of the hypertufa containers sets off the varied forms and colors of alpines and rock plants to perfection.

I first saw these containers in their traditional settings in English rock gardens, where they often are set among natural outcrops of rock and stone. It's hard to distinguish the hypertufa containers from real stone sinks and troughs. Usually rectangular, from two to four feet long and not quite as wide, with sharp edges and weathered surfaces, and set on stone pedestals or concrete blocks, they look like pocket Stonehenges, and their angular planes serve as perfect foils to the sturdy little rock plants living in them. The containers seem as ancient as the stone and rock that surround them, and they lend a time-worn distinction to the gardens they inhabit.

The following information on tools, ingredients, recipes, molding, and weatherizing is for making plant containers, but the process can be adapted to make birdbaths, stepping stones, and water basins as well (see p. 154).

MAKING HYPERTUFA CONTAINERS

A basement or garage which is heated and dry, and where it doesn't matter if the floor gets wet, is the best working area for making hypertufa containers.

MOLDS

For making small hypertufa containers, use old metal or rubber dishpans, kitty-litter trays, old plastic plant containers, or any other item that has the size you require and an interesting shape. These types of molds work well because they are light, portable, and reusable. You often can find interesting molds at garage sales and secondhand stores.

For larger troughs, visit hardware or feed-and-seed stores; rubber troughs for mixing cement and livestock feeding and watering containers shape up into handsome molds.

Ingredients

The basic ingredients in hypertufa mixture are cement, sand, and peat moss.

CEMENT

Use portland cement rather than pre-mix cement, since pre-mix contains gravel and therefore results in a coarse and unnatural texture on the finished container.

Sand

Mason's sand is preferable to coarser grades of sand because it bonds more strongly to the cement. Perlite is often substituted for sand because it is much lighter (an empty 12" x 13" x 5" container made with sand weighs approximately 20 pounds, so this is a major consideration) and because it gives a different, more nubbly texture to the finished container. Containers made with perlite look less like natural stone than ones made with sand to me, but this is a matter of taste, and you may like to try both materials in order to compare their finished textures.

Peat Moss

Use milled peat moss and sift it to remove unmilled chunks or sticks of wood.

Concrete Colorants

These powders come in various shades of brown, black, yellow, and green, and may be used to warm up the cold grey color of the cement; they can be purchased at building supply stores. Start out using just a pinch of colorant, or a few grains of several different colorants combined, for each batch of mixture you make. (Using more than a pinch per batch has left me with finished containers that glow in the dark.)

Proportions

The texture of a finished tufa depends upon the proportions of cement, sand, and peat moss used to make it. For instance, the following recipe results in a porous texture like tufa:

- 1 part portland cement
- 1 part mason's sand or perlite
- 2 parts milled peat moss

This recipe results in a denser texture like sandstone:

- 1 part cement
- 1½ parts sand
- 1½ parts peat moss

If you decide to experiment with different proportions of ingredients from the ones given here, measure the materials by volume rather than by weight.

Mixing and Molding

Now that all the ingredients and equipment are gathered, you are ready to start making hypertufa containers.

1. Cover the molds with thin sheets of plastic (plastic garbage bags work well) wherever they might come in contact with the hypertufa mixture. This will prevent the mixture from sticking to the sides of the mold as it dries.

Tools and Equipment

- thick rubber gloves, preferably with extra-long sleeves
- container to measure ingredients (an old two-gallon bucket with quantities in quarts printed on the side is good)
- large, shallow container for mixing hypertufa ingredients together
- watering can with spout
- plastic garbage bags, medium or large size
- molds (see note on molds on p. 150)
- short dowels with at least ½-inch diameter
- wire brush
- chisel
- optional: fibermesh; or ¼-inch hardware cloth, wire, and tinsnips for a reinforcement basket (see the box on p. 153)

2. Mix the milled peat moss and sand (or perlite) together. Then add the cement and mix well again. At this point you can add the concrete colorants.

3. Once all the dry ingredients are mixed together, start adding water a little at a time, and continue to add it slowly and to blend it into the mixture thoroughly after each addition. Make the mixture fairly dry, just enough to bind the materials together.

4. Start filling the bottom of the mold until the mixture is 1½ inches deep. Press the mixture down quite firmly to eliminate air holes or pockets. Then use the short dowels to carve out drainage holes. Next, build walls two inches thick, firmly packing the hypertufa to the mold walls.

5. Let the container sit and dry for 48 hours. If the weather is especially hot or dry, check the container after 24 hours. If you used a wet mixture, the container may take several days to semiharden. You are waiting for the container to be dry enough to handle, but not so dry that it is hard to "weatherize." It is ready when, as Mr. Lincoln Foster, premier alpinist and rock gardener says, the surface is "so firm that it cannot be dented with a finger but still soft enough to be scratched with a fingernail."

6. Weatherizing the container is a satisfying step because it gives hypertufa the texture and character of worn stone. First, unmold the semihard container and remove any plastic sheeting which sticks to it. Then, in order to make the gouges and chisel marks characteristic of real stone troughs and sinks, take a blunt object like a chisel and gouge and bash the container with it. (Some days, when the dog has just used a prized shrub for a chewing stick, for instance, this seems like a lot of fun.) After you have gouged and chiseled the container, take a wire brush and scour it. Finally, brush off any clinging bits of sand or other debris with an old paintbrush and then set the container where it can cure undisturbed for several weeks. Avoid placing containers in direct sunlight, or in temperatures below freezing until they have fully cured, usually in about a month to six weeks.

7. Freshly cured containers are still too "hot" from the chemicals released in the wetted cement to plant up. In order to neutralize the chemicals, take containers that have been curing for a minimum of four weeks in a heated space, and place them outside where they can be washed by the rain (or by hose water) for several weeks. Or use potassium of permanganate crystals, which are available at industrial-chemical supply stores, to speed up the process of neutralizing the cement. Mix the crystals with water to produce a Chianti-colored solution that is brushed over the surface of the container and allowed to sit for several hours before being hosed off. Dispose of the used solution away from animals and plants.

Reinforcement

Hypertufa containers are often reinforced with hardware cloth for extra structural strength. I don't use reinforcement on containers that are smaller in outside dimensions than 22 inches long by 17 inches wide by six inches deep. Reinforcing small containers is relatively costly, time-consuming, and in my experience counterproductive, because the hardware cloth sometimes prevents proper bonding between walls and corners. (Small troughs that will be moved around a great deal or used in harsh climates, where alternate freezes and thaws are common in the winter, may need reinforcement, however.)

Troughs having larger dimensions than those listed above probably need reinforcement, for which you can use either hardware cloth or a polypropylene reinforcing product called fibermesh. Fibermesh is easier to use than hardware cloth, and, because it is a filament that distributes equally throughout the trough, you don't have problems with improper bonding or subsequent flaking, as with the hardware cloth.

To strengthen your troughs with hardware cloth, use tinsnips to make a basket (from ¼-inch hardware cloth) that exactly centers on the walls and bottom of the trough. For example, a tradi-

tionally sized large trough has outer dimensions of 36" x 20" x 8" and walls that are two inches thick. This trough will need a basket that is 34" x 18" x 6" that has been cut from a single piece of hardware cloth and wired on the sides (Figure 10–1). Once you have filled the bottom of the mold with hypertufa about one inch deep, place the hardware cloth basket on top of the mixture and center it inside the mold.

To reinforce your troughs with fibermesh, first purchase it at a lumberyard or concrete supply store. Then, to a mixture of equal parts cement, peat moss, and perlite, add ¼ cup of fibermesh per gallon of mix, and stir all the materials together thoroughly. Add water as in step 3 and continue to make the trough following the directions in steps 4 through 7. (The fibermesh will stick out of the trough in stubs at this point.) After the trough has weathered and cured, burn off the extraneous fibermesh with a propane torch.

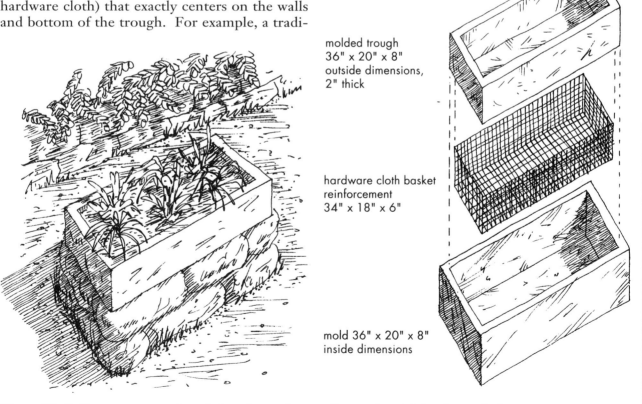

molded trough
36" x 20" x 8"
outside dimensions,
2" thick

hardware cloth basket
reinforcement
34" x 18" x 6"

mold 36" x 20" x 8"
inside dimensions

Figure 10–1. For extra strength, reinforce larger hypertufa troughs with hardware cloth.

Making Stepping Stones, Birdbaths, and Water Basins

You can make stepping stones and birdbaths from hypertufa mixture using the following recipe: one part cement, to one part sand, to one part peat moss.

To make a mold for stepping stones, take a fiberglass strip about two inches wide and 52 inches long and bend it into a circle that has a circumference of 48 inches and an overlap of four inches. Drill holes through both strips of fiberglass in the overlap area and thread wing-nut screws through them so the mold can be tightened when it is being filled with hypertufa mix, and then loosened when the stepping stone is to be unmolded, much like a springform baking pan. This mold is reusable.

Place the mold on a flat portable surface, such as a piece of plywood, and cover it with a sheet of plastic. Fill the mold at least 1½ inches deep with a fairly dry mix and press down firmly. You can trace designs on the wet mixture at this point if you wish to decorate your stepping stones. Stepping stones cure at a faster rate than containers, but leave them to harden for three or four weeks before placing them in foot-traffic areas, because they need to be sufficiently strong to bear a person's weight. Stepping stones made of hypertufa look especially nice placed flush with the earth in flower beds, or set in gravel if they are decorated with a Japanese motif. (To make a millstone, carve out a rough hole in the center of your stepping stone while the mix is still wet.)

Molds for birdbaths can be as simple as an old garbage can lid covered with plastic, or the dish of a birdbath with a shape you like. Use a fairly dry mix and mold, cure, and weatherize the birdbath as you would a hypertufa container. When finished, the birdbaths have a look of pleasantly worn stone, and can be nestled under overhanging shrubs or at the base of a tree.

Another unconventional use for hypertufa containers is to make them into water basins. Mold a relatively small container, one with outer dimensions of 12" x 13", for example, and make the walls quite thick, at least three inches wide, with a rounded inner opening. After weathering and curing the basin, position it about two-thirds of its length into the ground. We placed such a basin under a fatsia shrub, nestled by hostas, in a narrow passageway filled with bamboo and ferns, and the area now has the feeling of a small Japanese courtyard, complete with stone water basin. There is a pink-flowering camellia nearby, and we float its blossoms in the basin every spring.

PLANTING HYPERTUFA CONTAINERS

When I first saw hypertufa troughs in England, their textures and shapes were so intriguing that the alpines and rock plants inside them held a lesser interest for me at the time.

But once I had returned home and made half a dozen containers, the question of what to plant in them naturally came up. Besides filling them up with alpines and rock plants, I decided to try other types of plants in the hypertufa containers as well.

Some of the compact, low-growing herbs seemed like a good choice to start with, especially those having a grey or dusty green color, which looks attractive next to the weatherbeaten exterior of the containers, or ones whose compact forms are set off dramatically by the containers' sharp lines and angles. Most of these herbs also like a dry soil that is not too rich, an environment that is easy to create in hypertufa containers.

I planted up a couple of the containers with woolly thyme *(Thymus pseudolanuginosis)* and rupturewort *(Herniaria glabra)*, which liked their hypertufa environment so well that they crawled over the sides of the containers and down into the cracks between the bricks below them. These containers are sitting on the edge of a hot and sunny terrace near a patch of lavender, chives, and sage, and their stony texture helps create the effect of a rocky Mediterranean hillside covered in herbs in one corner of our Pacific Northwest garden.

We also planted some containers with flowering plants that have leaves similar in shape and texture to the low-growing herbs, such as Cheddar pinks *(Dianthus gratianopolitanus)*, stringy stonecrop *(Sedum lineare)*, and snow-in-summer *(Cerastium tomentosum)*. These plants will surge over the sides of the containers as the growing season progresses, and they look especially nice placed on the top of a low, wide wall, where they can spill out of the containers and down over the wall below. They also can be placed near herb patches to add color and complementary foliage to the larger plants.

Blooms with warm tints — pinks, reds, creams, and lemon yellow — seem to show off the color and texture of hypertufa containers to their best advantage, and there are many plants with flowers in these colors that could be added to our list, among them thrift *(Armeria maritima)*, moss campion *(Silene schafta)*, aubretia (especially *Aubrieta deltoidea* 'Red Carpet'), candytuft *(Iberis sempervirens)*, and myrtle euphorbia *(Euphorbia myrsinites)*. Rampant growers, or plants so tall that they dwarf the containers, should be avoided, however.

We like to position containers with flowering plants where they can be seen from inside the house. When their time of bloom is over, we move them back to a spot where their leaf form and texture complements the surrounding plants, and bring out another container whose plants are beginning to bloom. This continual movement of containers helps to make the garden a dynamic landscape which never seems static or stale.

A Pacific Northwest garden nearly always has a cool, shady, and moist corner in it, and we have used hypertufa containers in such areas with mosses and selaginellas planted in them. Mosses love hypertufa and will grow on its surface naturally in rainy climates. In areas where mosses are not so invasive, you can encourage their growth on the containers by pouring buttermilk over the hypertufa and gently pressing small patches of moss onto it. Keep the surface moist and shaded until the moss is looking robust, then place the container in a part of your garden which duplicates as closely as possible the original growing conditions of the moss.

In dappled shade areas, you can plant hypertufa containers with Scotch moss (*Sagina subulata* 'Aurea', not a true moss), a lime-green mat sporting starry flowers that is guaranteed to light up any spot it is placed in, no matter how dark and dreary.

Another plant for light shade is a favorite of mine, pink saxifrage (*Saxifraga rosacea*, the pink variety) — a cushiony mound of short, fleshy leaves that is covered in spring by wiry flower stalks six inches high. The stalks support flowers of a bright, deep pink that really sings against the grey of hypertufa. And when the flowers fade, the fresh, light green leaves still look handsome against the containers for the rest of the summer.

All of the plants listed above are relatively easy to grow in containers. The sun-lovers like a fast-draining soil, which you can provide by adding equal measures of washed sand and perlite to the potting soil, by placing a ½-inch layer of gravel or stone on the bottom of the container before adding the amended potting soil, and by raising the containers off the ground on bricks or blocks to encourage rapid draining after watering. After planting the containers, cover the soil with turkey grit (available in feed-and-seed stores) which acts as a mulch. The shade-lovers benefit from being planted in a soil amended with peat moss and leaf mold.

The planted hypertufa container I am most fond of in our garden (and the one most visitors seem to enjoy, too) is wide and shallow and contains a small piece of volcanic rock, several hens-and-chickens *(Echeveria elegans)*, and a bronzy, fleshy sedum which we bought without a nametag on the plant rack outside the local hardware store. Hypertufa containers display common and humble plants to their best advantage as effectively as they showcase rare and precious ones, and for this reason we continue to experiment with new plants in our containers every year.

Several years ago I started using hypertufa containers as planters for bonsai that were in the first stages of shaping and training. The containers are deeper, and more rough and unfinished than the elegant ceramic dishes usually used in displaying bonsai. But even if the hypertufa containers are untraditional, they somehow look appropriate. Perhaps it is because their texture brings to mind the rock and stone outcrops found in mountain landscapes near the ancient trees that bonsai are meant to evoke. Two years later, the fledgling bonsai are thriving in their hypertufa pots, and the moss which bewhiskers the hypertufa surface has spread over their exposed roots.

GLOSSARY

allée: a straight-edged path bordered by trees or shrubs; usually constructed in formal gardens.

alpine: mountain terrain located between the timberline and the year-round snowline; native habitat of alpine plants.

ashlar: any kind of cut and shaped stone used in outdoor construction.

batter: the inward slope of a wall from base to top; ensures structural stability.

basalt: a fine-grained igneous rock, strong and weather-resistant; used in garden walls, and as stepping stones and specimen rocks.

Belgian blocks: paving units, often approximately the size and dimensions of a large brick. They are made of granite or other durable stone, and are used to construct paths and terraces.

berm: a low, artificially made mound of earth which adds height and depth to a flat landscape; often used in rock gardens, landscaped with rocks and plants.

cobblestones: naturally rounded stones with dimensions between two and 12 inches; used in paths, terraces, xeriscapes, and water features.

coping: the final horizontal layer of stones that cap and waterproof a stone wall; usually wide and shallow, coping stones are often mortared into place.

courses: the horizontal layers of stones used in constructing a stone wall.

crazy paving: irregularly edged flagstones which are used to construct paths and terraces with an informal look.

crushed rock: stones approximately ¼ inch to two inches in size which have been mechanically crushed; characterized by sharply angled corners and irregular planes, crushed rock packs together well and is useful as a foundation material for stone constructions.

decomposed granite: a granular, naturally rounded gravel often used in Japanese dry gardens.

dolmen: a prehistoric structure made of massive upright and horizontal stones; found in Britain, Ireland, and France.

drain rock: naturally rounded stones between ⅞ inch and two inches in diameter; often used in xeriscapes and water features.

dry wall: a stone wall constructed without mortar, which depends on gravity and the fit between the stones for its stability.

flagstone: any kind of stone which splits into shallow slabs suitable for paving.

footing: the foundation of a wall.

gneiss: a medium- to coarse-grained metamorphic rock; strong and weather-resistant, it is most often used in garden walls and rockeries.

granite: a fine- to medium-coarse–grained igneous stone; dense and water-resistant, it is often used in garden walls, and as stepping stones and specimen rocks.

gravel: naturally rounded or mechanically crushed stones ranging in size from ¼ inch to 1½ inches. Often used in gravel gardens, paths, terraces, and water features.

hypertufa: a mixture of cement, sand, and peat moss, which can be molded and weathered to look like natural stone. Used for making plant containers, stepping stones, etc.

igneous rock: rock formed from solidified minerals and gases originally found within the earth's crust.

lattice wall: a wall featuring decorative openings in regular or random patterns.

limestone: a fine- to coarse-grained sedimentary rock; often used as ashlar or flagstone because it splits easily, limestone also serves as the preferred rock for constructing rock gardens.

marble: a fine-grained metamorphic rock that is strong and weather-resistant; more often used in indoor than outdoor paving and walls because of its cost and its slickness when wet.

metamorphic rock: igneous, sedimentary, or other metamorphic rocks that have been transformed by heat, pressure, or chemical action into other kinds of stone.

mortar: a mixture of cement and fine aggregates, such as sand, lime, or fireclay, that is used to bind paving and wall units together. When using mortar in stone constructions, use fireclay in place of lime, since lime stains stone.

outcrops: bare rock formations protruding from the surrounding soil.

pea gravel: a fine grade of naturally rounded stones approximately ¼ inch in diameter; used in gravel gardens and as flooring for children's play areas.

Pennsylvania bluestone: a flagstone used to make attractive, durable paving for terraces and paths.

pergola: a garden passageway made of stone, brick,

or wooden columns that support an overhead trellis on which vines are trained.

retaining wall: a wall that holds earth in place vertically; a retaining wall can either be mortared or dry-laid.

rubble: uncut stone.

sandstone: a fine- to coarse-grained sedimentary rock that splits easily; often used in the construction of garden walls and paths.

scree: an accumulation of angular rock fragments found at the base of a cliff or steep slope; often replicated in rock gardens, where its stony "soil" accommodates a variety of alpines and rock plants.

sedimentary rock: rock composed from the consolidated debris of igneous, metamorphic, and other sedimentary rock; because they split easily, sedimentary stones such as limestone and sandstone are used extensively in garden constructions.

slate: a fine-grained metamorphic stone that is highly weather-resistant; sometimes used as flagstones in constructing garden paths and terraces.

strata: horizontal layers of rock.

stretcher stones: long stones laid parallel to the face of a wall to add stability.

tie stones: long stones laid across the width of the wall to add lateral stability.

veneer: a course of stone added to the surface of a wall as decoration.

watercourse: an artificial channel for a stream; constructed most often in formal gardens.

weep holes: through-wall drainage holes used to prevent water from backing up behind retaining walls.

wythes: vertical stacks of stones in a wall that are one stone wide.

BIBLIOGRAPHY

Chinese and Japanese Gardens

Davidson, A. K. *The Art of Zen Gardening.* Los Angeles: Jeremy P. Tarcher, Inc., 1983.

Du Wan. *Stone Catalogue of Cloudy Forest*, trans. Edward H. Shafer. Berkeley and Los Angeles: University of California Press, 1961.

Engel, David H. *Creating a Chinese Garden.* Portland: Timber Press, 1986.

Graham, Dorothy. *Chinese Gardens.* New York: Dodd, Mead & Co., 1938.

Ji, Cheng. *The Craft of Gardens*, trans. Alison Hardie. New Haven: Yale University Press, 1988.

Keswick, Maggie. *The Chinese Garden: History, Art & Architecture.* New York: St. Martin's Press, 1986.

Morris, Edwin T. *The Gardens of China: History, Art, and Meanings.* New York: Charles Scribner's Sons, 1983.

Newsom, Samuel. *A Japanese Garden Manual for Westerners: Basic Design and Construction.* Tokyo: Tokyo News Service, 1965.

Saito, Katsuo. *Japanese Gardening Hints.* Tokyo: Japan Publications Inc., 1969.

Sawyers, Claire. Brooklyn Botanic Garden Series. *Japanese Gardens.* New York: Brooklyn Botanic Garden Inc., 1985.

Siren, Osvald. *Gardens of China.* New York: Ronald Press, 1949.

Tsu, Frances Ya-sing. *Landscape Design in Chinese Gardens.* New York: McGraw-Hill, 1988.

Yang, Hongxun. *The Classical Gardens of China.* New York: Van Nostrand Reinhold Co., 1982.

Western Gardens

Art, Henry W. *The Wildflower Gardener's Guide: California, Desert Southwest, and Northern Mexico Edition.* Pownal, Vermont: Garden Way Publishing, 1990.

—. *The Wildflower Gardener's Guide: Midwest, Great Plains, and Canadian Prairies Edition.* Pownal, Vermont: Garden Way Publishing, 1991.

—. *The Wildflower Gardener's Guide: Northeast, Mid-Atlantic, Great Lakes, and Eastern Canada Edition.* Pownal, Vermont: Garden Way Publishing, 1987.

—. *The Wildflower Gardener's Guide: Pacific Northwest, Rocky Mountain, and Western Canada Edition.* Pownal, Vermont: Garden Way Publishing, 1990.

Bernbaum, Edwin. *Sacred Mountains of the World.* San Francisco: Sierra Club Books, 1990.

Brookes, John. *Gardens of Paradise: The History and Design of the Great Islamic Gardens.* New York: New Amsterdam, 1987.

Carl, Joachim. *Miniature Gardens.* Portland: Timber Press, 1981.

Colborn, Nigel. *Leisurely Gardening.* North Pomfret, Vermont: Trafalgar Square/David and Charles, 1989.

Edwards, A. E. *Rock Gardens.* London: Ward, Lock & Co., 4th Ed., 1954.

Elliott, Brent. *Victorian Gardens.* Portland: Timber Press, 1986.

Farrer, Reginald. *My Rock Garden.* London: E. Arnold, 1907.

Foster, H. Lincoln. *Rock Gardening.* Portland: Timber Press, 1982.

Gibbons, Bob and Liz. *Creating a Wildlife Garden.* London: Hamlyn Publishing Group, 1988.

Hadfield, Miles. *The Art of the Garden.* New York: E.P. Dutton and Co., 1965.

Martin, Laura C. *The Wildflower Meadow Book: A Gardener's Guide.* Charlotte, North Carolina: East Woods Press, 1986.

Moynihan, Elizabeth B. *Paradise as a Garden in Persia and Mughal India.* New York: George Braziller, 1979.

Osler, Mirabel. *A Gentle Plea for Chaos.* New York: Simon and Schuster, 1989.

Page, Russell. *The Education of a Gardener.* New York: Vintage Books, 1985.

Rose, Graham. *The Romantic Garden.* New York: Penguin Books, 1988.

Saudan, Michel, and Sylvia Saudan-Skira. *From Folly to Follies.* New York: Abbeville Press, 1987.

Saville, Diana. *Walled Gardens: Their Planting and Design.* London: Batsford, 1982.

Schenck, George. *How to Plan, Establish, and Maintain Rock Gardens.* Menlo Park, California: Lane Book Company, 1964.

Stevenson, Violet. *The Wild Garden.* New York: Penguin Handbooks, 1985.

Thacker, Christopher. *The History of Gardens.* Berkeley: University of California Press, 1979.

Wilson, William H.W. *Landscaping with Wildflowers and Native Plants.* San Ramon, California: Ortho Books, 1984.

INDEX

(Illustrations are indicated by page numbers in *italics*;
charts and tables are indicated by page numbers in **bold.**)